Rental Homes

The Tax Shelter That Works and Grows for You

Rental Homes

The Tax Shelter That Works and Grows for You

Vincent William Zucchero

Attorney at Law
1801 Wilshire Boulevard, Suite A
Santa Monica, California 90403
(213) 348-2903

Reston Publishing Company, Inc.
Reston, Virginia
A Prentice-Hall Company

Library of Congress Cataloging in Publication Data

Zucchero, Vincent William.
  Rental homes.

  Includes index.
  1. Rental housing.   2. Real estate investment.
  3. Real property tax.   4. Tax shelters.
  I. Title.
  HD1394.Z82   1983   343.7305'23   82-10197
  ISBN 0-8359-6644-5   347.303523

Copyright 1981, 1983 by
Vincent William Zucchero

Reston Publishing Company, Inc.
Reston, Virginia 22090

NOTE that while this volume has been prepared primarily with regard to federal law, when state law was applicable, California laws were used in the absence of contrary language. You should consult professionals in your area to ascertain differences in local laws and the tax ramifications due to those laws.

NOTE regarding usage of the masculine gender: The generic usage of masculine nouns and pronouns to depict individuals throughout this volume is intended to provide additional clarity and improve textual continuity, while reducing quantity. No social statement is intended thereby by the author or the publisher.

10 9 8 7 6 5 4 3 2 1

Printed in the United States of America

*To my family and friends,
who have always been there
when I needed them.*

Contents

PART IV: DISPOSITION OF REAL PROPERTY

Preface

Let's face it—since 1913, the Federal Government has had the power to tax our incomes. The Government has been so successful that these taxes represent the largest deduction from our paychecks.

Many people have tried varying schemes to reduce these taxes, such as claiming the Fifth Amendment (that the information on the tax form could be self-incriminating, once signed); claiming tax-exempt status as a minister or religious organization; claiming that the dollar is worthless (since it is not backed by gold, silver, or other tangible substance) and, thus, is not money at all; claiming income taxes are illegal or unconstitutional; and so on.

All of these claims have been rejected by the Internal Revenue Service and nearly all have already resulted in criminal prosecution and conviction. In addition, civil penalties are possible. Recently, the IRS has pushed for larger penalties. For example, the interest rate on deficiencies is based on the prime rate, not 90% of prime, as before. Further, beginning January 1, 1983, the rate will be adjusted and set annually, as opposed to the present rule which prevents the rate from being established more often than once every 23 months.

Just to show you how badly the odds are stacked against persons employing the aforementioned means, 265 people have been convicted in the past 2½ years for their "protest" activities. Only 12 persons were acquitted. Of those convicted, 55% received jail sentences in excess of one year. As of this writing, nearly 400 persons are under criminal investigation for alleged illegal "protest" activities. Literally thousands of returns are examined each year for suspected "protest" actions.

It is not difficult to recognize that, for most Americans, the Government is and will essentially be your business partner. If you receive wages, you know that you will work sometime into May of each year before those hard-earned wages effectively begin to flow into your pocket. The tax system, being progressive in nature, penalizes incentive as you struggle to increase your income while the built-in (marginal tax) bracket creep not only negates the increase, but can actually cause you to owe more than you received (in percentage terms). It is unfair, but the system is not likely to be changed in the near future.

Does that mean that we are doomed to paying high federal income taxes for life? No, not by a long shot. The common thread in most illegal tax reduction schemes is tax evasion, which is severely punished. However, *tax avoidance* is a desirable concept and acceptable to the Internal Revenue Service. Tax avoidance is merely complying with tax law and taking advantage of what the law gives us, which, in many cases is considerable, as you will see later in this guide.

For example, the Government has various social and economic goals that it seeks to further in an optimum manner. In this regard, as an incentive to stimulate the growth of the housing stock in this country, the Government provides additional deductions to the taxpayer, thus attracting private investment dollars to this area. So, instead of the Government having to provide 100% of the financing for this growth, it only has to provide one-half, assuming the taxpayer is in the 50% tax bracket.

Therefore, our task is first to recognize the goals the Government seeks to further and, second, to utilize fully all the tax incentives offered. In the subsequent pages I will be addressing the aforementioned goal of the Government (more residential housing). In doing so, I will explore and take advantage of all tax benefits which accrue. And, while you, the taxpayer, are reducing your income taxes, other significant benefits inure to you by use of the described method:

1. You, to a great extent, will be using other peoples' money to increase your own wealth and will be using your own increasing funds for other purposes.

2. You will be amassing a large net worth.

3. You will be using inflation to your advantage, instead of dying by it.

4. You can properly provide for your retirement.

With regard to the latter point, and in light of all of the recent publicity, most of us know of the sad shape of our Social Security System. Many of you who are presently working and paying a significant percentage of your paychecks in return for a promise of payment of future retirement benefits have realized that you probably will not see much, if any, of those dollars upon retirement. Thus, you would be wise to recognize that there is a legitimate need for private retirement (income) planning. This must be done now, while you are in your wealth-building prime.

I am not advocating quitting your job, nor stopping payment of taxes outright, nor eliminating your "contributions" to the Social Security System. However, it does seem reasonable to follow the old adage, "Let your *money* work for you, instead of *you* working for your money." The program outlined in the following chapters is but one means to do this. And, I believe it is the most effective for the greatest number of people.

What I am about to describe is not a get-rich quick scheme, but a proven tax shelter device that has been employed by the wealthy for a long time. Now *you* can make use of it. In fact, due to the progressiveness of the tax rates, as I alluded to earlier, it would appear that tax shelters actually favor moderate income persons over the wealthy. By way of illustration, look at the representative tax table on page xvi. It indicates overall tax liability by taxable income range, along with the respective marginal tax rate.

Assume a married couple, filing jointly, had a taxable income of $40,000. Assume that they were able to reduce this amount by 20% (to $32,000) by use of tax shelter devices. As shown in the tax table, their marginal tax rate would decline from 39% to 33%. However, a taxpayer and his wife earning a taxable income of $80,000, with the same 20% tax shelter reduction, would not even get a change in their 49% marginal rate. These results occur because most of the increase in marginal rates is in the *moderate* income brackets.

Of course, while reducing the tremendous impact of income taxes is our aim, it is not our only goal. We are not satisfied only to reduce taxable income. Within our tax shelter framework, we want to maximize after-tax cash flow. After all, the idea is not to actually lose money but to report legitimate losses which then can be used against income received, thus lowering taxable income and effec-

TAX RATE SCHEDULE°
Married Individuals Filing Jointly

Taxable Income		Income Tax Liability			
Over	Not Exceeding	Base Tax	+	Marginal Rates, %	On Excess Over
—	$ 3,400	—		—	—
$ 3,400	5,500	—		12	$ 3,400
5,500	7,600	$ 252		14	5,500
7,600	11 900	546		16	7,600
11,900	16,000	1,234		19	11,900
16,000	20,200	2,013		22	16,000
20,200	24,600	2,937		25	20,200
24,600	29,900	4,037		29	24,600
29,900	35,200	5,574		33	29,900
35,200	45,800	7,323		39	35,200
45,800	60,000	11,457		44	45,800
60,000	85,600	17,705		49	60,000
85,600	—	30,249		50	85,600

°Reflects Economic Recovery Tax Act of 1981 marginal rate reductions. Table used in determining federal income taxes for the year 1982.

tively providing more cash in your pocket. In fact, the definition of a good tax shelter is a situation when a person's taxable income is less than his cash flow. An *excellent* tax shelter—something for which we will strive—is when reportable tax losses offset income from *other* sources. This level can be reached.

To be sure, the program outlined in this guide requires some effort on your part. After all, there are no free lunches! However, this may be the closest yet. The described method is immediately available to some of you, and given time, is not out of reach of any motivated individual. By reading this guide, you have already taken the first step in your quest to reduce your income taxes, increase your wealth, and hopefully lead a freer, happier life. Good luck the rest of the way!

Disclaimer

The reader purchases and reads this guide with the understanding that the author and publisher specifically disclaim any liability, loss, or risk, personal or otherwise, which may result as a consequence, directly or indirectly, of the use or application of the contents of this work.

The author is not recommending any specific program for the taxpayer, only describing one method to reduce taxes. In addition, the author is not attempting to sell or offer to sell investments of any kind. Further, the guide is not meant to constitute a solicitation or prospectus.

The reader should consult competent advisors to help choose his strategy. Qualified financial planners which include some attorneys, accountants, insurance persons, investment counselors, real estate agents/brokers, and the like can assist the reader in selecting a proper tax reduction method as part of the taxpayer's overall financial plan.

This guide, and the information therein does not constitute legal, tax, or financial planning advice. The reader should not rely on the legal, tax, and financial material contained herein. Instead, the reader should consult his own attorney, accountant, and financial planner for investment, legal, and/or tax advice regarding any tax reduction or other financial plan.

The reader should be aware that the examples in the guide are hypothetical. Any program on which the reader embarks may or may not perform similarly and, thus, the reader should not undertake a tax reduction program solely on this basis. Any similarity between material appearing in this guide and any present, past, or future method is purely coincidental.

Current tax law has been utilized in the preparation of the material in the guide. I have attempted to avoid errors in law or fact and, to this end, the material has been reviewed by professionals in the legal, accounting, and real estate fields. Since the tax law is continually changing, every effort will be made to keep future editions current. Errors, if any, should be brought to the attention of the author, in care of the publisher.

The material in this guide has not been reviewed by the Internal Revenue Service or any other governmental agency.

Overview

All of us are paying more taxes than we would like and, probably, most of us are paying more than we need to. There are ways to reduce income, gift, and estate taxes or, possibly, to eliminate those taxes—quite legally. In fact, the Internal Revenue Code encourages the method I am going to describe to you. And, in reducing taxes, many additional benefits accrue and are a direct result of the use of this method.

It is important to realize that the immediate availability of this technique will vary with your current economic circumstances. But, over time, most of you reading this guide should be able to cut your taxes significantly.

This technique is *not* to be characterized as a method for buying and selling real property, *nor* as a method of holding property for the production of income. In fact, you will want to treat the ownership and operation of your real properties as a "trade or business" as classified by the Internal Revenue Code. You will rent these properties out on an ongoing basis, and you will be accumulating circumstantial evidence that your involvement is a "trade or business" by doing a variety of things that will be discussed later. The purpose of distinguishing your involvement may seem meaningless at this point but, in terms of the Code, it is quite important because you will want to preserve all deductions and tax benefits available to you—and there are potentially more of these if you are operating the properties as a "trade or business" than otherwise.

So, What Is This Technique?

Those of you who presently own a personal residence have some feeling for what I am about to say. *However,* present home ownership is *not* a prerequisite to following this technique. You know that home ownership provides the owner with significant tax deductions. Typical of these personal deductions are interest and real property taxes. More importantly, the magnitude of these deductions permits you, the taxpayer-owner, to exceed the "zero bracket amount" and, thus, itemize these deductions. The "zero bracket amount" (formerly the "standard deduction") is built into the tax schedules, and amounts to $3,400 for married couples filing jointly and $2,300 for single individuals. It is less likely in a normal case, without home ownership, that you will have itemized deductions (medical, state and local taxes, interest, charity, casualty, miscellaneous) which approximate the zero bracket amount. Thus, these potential deductions, while significant and legitimate amounts expended, are wasted and useless and, in effect, you only receive benefit of the zero bracket amount. However, if you have $3,401 (married, filing jointly) or $2,301 (single individual) or more of these deductions, you should itemize, because any excess over the applicable zero bracket amount will yield tax benefit. This is so because these excess deductions will directly offset ordinary income. More than likely, with home ownership, you will greatly exceed the zero bracket amount and, thus, will derive a significant tax advantage since you will be utilizing the zero bracket amount *and* the amount of excess deductions against your income.

Let me illustrate the difference in federal income tax liability with and without ownership of a personal residence. Assume in this example that a married couple, filing jointly, had a combined gross income last year of $35,000. They are both under 65 years old and had two minor children living at home in California. They had potential net medical, charity, and miscellaneous deductions of $400, as well as a potential general sales tax deduction of $400. In addition, they had potential deductions of $938 for state and local taxes, $100 for auto licenses, and $1,000 for interest on charge accounts and auto loans. Note that these potential deductions amount to $2,848, falling short of the $3,400 zero bracket amount.

Thus, the taxpayers could not itemize and these $2,848 potential deductions were wasted. The federal income taxes in this case would have been approximately $6,525.

However, if the couple had purchased a home, say four years ago, with a mortgage of approximately $53,000 at a 9% (9¼% APR) interest, the result would have been quite different. The interest on the mortgage would have been $4,700, and the real property taxes would have been $800 annually. In this case, the federal income taxes would have been approximately $4,911, a difference of $1,614! The calculations are as follows:

Case 1: No home ownership

Gross income/Adjusted gross income	$35,000
less personal exemptions	(4,000)
Taxable income	$31,000
FEDERAL INCOME TAX[a]	**$ 6,525**

Case 2: Ownership of personal residence

Gross income/Adjusted gross income			$35,000
less personal exemptions			(4,000)
less itemized deductions			
medical, charity, misc.		$ 400	
taxes			
state/local	$ 938		
real property	800		
general sales	400		
personal property	(N/A in CA)		
other (car license)	100		
Subtotal		$ 2,238	
interest			
home mortgage	$ 4,700		
charge cards, car	1,000		
Subtotal		$ 5,700	
Total itemized deductions		$ 8,338	
less zero bracket amount		(3,400)	
Excess itemized deductions			(4,938)
Taxable income			$26,062
FEDERAL INCOME TAX[a]			**$ 4,911**

[a]These amounts reflect the Economic Recovery Tax Act of 1981 income tax revisions.

Is That It?

No. What you *don't* get with ownership of your personal residence is what can make or break you financially and is what this guide, to a large extent, is all about. Because this is your personal residence, the Internal Revenue Service *does not* allow you certain deductions, such as depreciation, maintenance, and repairs, etc., as well as other tax benefits. It does permit these deductions and additional benefits if you own and operate rental real property as a trade or business. The depreciation deduction (discussed in Part II) alone allowed on a rental unit can very often offset a much larger portion of your income than the interest deduction you would receive. As an illustration, in the proforma at the end of Part II, a $60,000 rental home with a $48,000 first mortgage at 9¾% (10% APR) interest could yield a first year depreciation deduction of $6,120, while the interest deduction totals "only" $4,540.

Taking the $60,000 house just mentioned, let's compare first year total deductions attributable to the house only, if you rented the house out as opposed to using it as your personal residence.

Typical Deductions	Rental Property[a]	Personal Residence
Real Property Tax	$ 1,400	$ 1,400
Interest	4,540	4,540
Depreciation	6,120	Not Available
Operating Expenses	1,215	Not Available
TOTAL GROSS DEDUCTIONS	$13,275	$ 5,940
TOTAL NET DEDUCTIONS[b]	**$13,275**	**$ 2,540**

[a] *Note:* Additional income from rents results in this case. Therefore, the deductions in this case would shelter all of this rental income plus $7,575 of other income. In addition, you should be aware that the proforma at the end of Part II has been set up to reflect a negative pre-tax cash flow. It could have easily been established to reflect a break-even or positive pre-tax cash flow. (*Note:* The *after*-tax cash flow, the real key, is positive.)
[b] In the case of rental property with this type of program, these deductions are "trade or business" expenses, which are deducted undiminished from gross income. In the case of the personal residence, these deductions amount to personal itemized deductions from which must be subtracted the zero bracket amount (here $3,400) to yield excess itemized deductions. The minimum value results if the taxpayer has *no* other itemized deductions.

Comparing the deductions *after* the $5,700 of rent has been offset (see the previous table footnotes), the net available deductions when the house is used as a rental unit are at least $1,635 or 28% (and possibly as much as $5,035 or 198%) *greater* than if the house were used as a personal residence—all things being equal. When viewed in the aggregate, the house used as a rental unit yields at least $7,335 of additional deductions, or 123% *more* deductions, than the house used as a personal residence. (In the best case, the rental unit yields $10,735 of additional deductions or 423% more than the house used as a personal residence as seen in the following tables.)

Net Available Deductions

	Rental Property	Personal Residence	Difference When House Is Used as a Rental Property	
			Amount	Percent
Best Case	$7,575	$2,540	$5,035	198
Worst Case	$7,575	$5,940	$1,635	28

Total Deductions

	Rental Property	Personal Residence	Difference When House Is Used as a Rental Property	
			Amount	Percent
Best Case	$13,275	$2,540	$10,735	423
Worst Case	$13,275	$5,940	$ 7,335	123

The effect on your income taxes this year can be readily seen by comparing Cases 1 and 2.

As you can readily see, merely using the house as a rental unit instead of a personal residence will save approximately $599 in federal income taxes, not to speak of savings in state (California) income tax of $118. This occurs in spite of the fact that the taxpayer's gross income has increased by $5,700, and his after-tax spendable income by $5,152, a gain of 27.6%! (Again, for the sake of completeness, this example has used figures from the proforma at the end of Part II, indicating a pre-tax negative cash flow, which should decrease as rents increase. However, a break-even or positive

Case 1: Ownership of a $60,000 house used as a personal residence.

Gross income/Adjusted gross income[a]			$ 35,000
less personal exemptions			(4,000)
less itemized deductions			
medical, charity, misc.		$ 400	
taxes			
state/local	$ 907		
real property	1,400		
general sales	400		
personal property	(N/A in CA)		
other (car license)	100		
Subtotal		$ 2,807	
interest			
home mortgage[b]	$ 4,540		
charge cards, car	1,000		
Subtotal		$ 5,540	
Total itemized deductions		$ 8,747	
less zero bracket amount[a]		(3,400)	
Excess itemized deductions			(5,347)
Taxable income			$25,653
FEDERAL INCOME TAX[c]			$ 4,342

[a]Married couple filing jointly, both under 65 years old, with two minor children at home in California. [Assumes one spouse does not work. Otherwise, marriage penalty relief of 5% on 1982 returns (up to $1,500 of lower earning spouse's wages) is deducted from gross income. In 1983 and forward the deduction is 10% (up to $3,000).]
[b]$48,000 mortgage balance at 9¾% (10% APR) interest.
[c]Reflects Economic Recovery Tax Act of 1981 marginal tax rate changes.

cash flow program can easily be set up. The effects of various programs will be discussed later.)

Are You Getting Interested?

I hope so. The point is that the Internal Revenue Service *encourages* the ownership of real estate (especially income property used in a trade or business) as a tax-saving device because it furthers the objectives of the Government. In this case it aids in attracting private investment dollars to the housing industry and this, in turn, aids in providing more housing which is badly needed. Therefore, why not take the IRS up on its invitation?

If you operate these real estate purchases as a trade or business, legitimate deductions in the aforementioned categories are, gener-

Case 2: Ownership of a $60,000 house used as a rental unit

Gross income[a]		$ 40,700
Less "trade or business" expenses		
real property taxes	$ 1,400	
interest[b]	4,540	
depreciation	6,120	
other operating expenses	1,215	
Total		(13,275)
Adjusted gross income		$ 27,425

less excess itemized deductions			
medical, charity, misc.		$ 400	
taxes			
state/local	$ 789		
real property	-0-		
general sales	450		
personal property	(N/A in CA)		
other (car license)	100		
Subtotal		$ 1,339	
interest			
personal residence	-0-		
charge cards (car)	1,000		
Subtotal		$ 1,000	
Total itemized deductions		$ 2,739	
less zero bracket amount[a]		(3,400)	
Excess itemized deductions[c]		—	
less personal exemptions			(4,000)
Taxable income			$ 23,425
FEDERAL INCOME TAX[d]			**$ 3,743**

[a]Gross income includes $35,000 combined wages and $5,700 net rental income. Married couple filing jointly, both under 65 years of age, with two minor children living at home in California. See footnotes in Case 1.

[b]$48,000 mortgage balance at 9¾% (10% APR) interest.

[c]*Note:* Since itemized deductions do not exceed the zero bracket amount, the taxpayer should not itemize these deductions. Thus there is no deduction reflected for these amounts.

[d]Reflects Economic Recovery Tax Act of 1981 marginal tax rate changes.

ally speaking, unlimited in amount. You could literally reduce your income taxes to zero. No other legally approved activity, as far as the average working individual is concerned, is as beneficial taxwise at a similar risk level.

If that wasn't enough, compare rates of return over a two year period with, let's say, a certificate of deposit at a bank yielding 10% interest per year. (Assume in this illustration that the taxpayer is in a 50% tax bracket—something which is not hard to do today.)

After-Tax Rates of Return[a]

	Certificate of Deposit	$60,000 House As A Rental Unit, Then Sold[b]
Net Yield after taxes (50% rate)	10.25%	88.24%
Less Inflation (10% per year)	(21.00%)	(21.00%)
Net Yield over Inflation	(10.75%)	67.24%

[a]Over a two year period.
[b]See the detailed proforma at the end of Part II.

Because of the favorable tax treatment and the appreciation of real property, rates of return on real property (especially income-producing property) should consistently be higher than most other forms of investment, as in this case. In this illustration, if the taxpayer had purchased the 10% certificate of deposit, he actually would have fallen *behind* inflation by 10.75%. But the taxpayer who purchased a house, rented it out for two years, and then sold it, *gained* on inflation by a *plus* 67.24%. It will be difficult to match such a performance without getting into much more speculative and risky types of investments.

Risk Vs. Reward

The amount of financial reward is measured in dollars, but offsetting this reward is the risk associated with the particular investment. Generally, the higher the reward, the higher the risk and vice-versa.

Savings Deposits

At the lower end of the risk spectrum (and consequently the lower end of the reward spectrum) are savings deposits at federally chartered savings and loan/banks. The return might be 5 to 5½% pre-tax or 2½ to 2¾% after-tax if you are in the 50% tax bracket annually. However, your savings are insured up to $100,000 by the Federal Government and, thus, there is little risk associated with this form of investment.

Stocks/Bonds

Stocks/bonds have a little higher return—maybe at the high end, 10 to 18% pre-tax (or 5 to 9% after-tax) plus potential appreciation/ depreciation in price. Stocks/bonds held for at least a year do qualify for favorable capital gains treatment. However, these securities have some risk. If the particular industry in general has a bad year, or certain world/domestic events occur, the market can fluctuate rather dramatically. In addition, trading by large institutional investors (e.g., pension funds, etc.) can make or break a particular security. (Municipal bonds may offer tax-free yields of 9 to 10%, which translate into effective yields of 18 to 20%, assuming a 50% tax bracket. There is less risk with these bonds than with some other securities, but municipalities have been known to have been on the verge of bankruptcy—recall the recent problems in New York and Cleveland.)

Money Market Funds

Money market funds (where investors' money is pooled to buy short-term securities) can offer relatively high rates—recently as high as 17 to 18% (8½ to 9% after taxes). Although no federal agency insures these funds, their risk level is low since the underlying short-term investments are generally made in U.S. Treasury securities or high quality commercial paper. Additionally, these money market funds provide a high level of liquidity to investors. You can withdraw your funds without penalty by placing a phone call.

Second Trust Deeds

Second trust deeds yielding 19 to 25% pre-tax (or 9 to 12½% after-tax) are a bit riskier, except those trust deeds on properties located in markets with extremely rapid appreciation in real estate prices. However, even in these markets, many investors who provided funds for these second trust deed loans have lost their money because the value of the underlying security (the equity in the property) was insufficient to cover the loan. Recently, in California (a large second trust deed market), a number of mortgage brokerage firms have been charged with fraud.

Metals Markets

Gold and silver had meteoric rises in price in the early months of 1980, only to decline sharply later in the same year, causing losses to a significant number of people. The metals markets play on world crises and haven't been the same since the 1980 events. In addition, these markets are subject to manipulative attempts by a few individuals who can make or break the market—and they usually do not tell the rest of us when they are going to act!

Commodities and Oil/Gas

Commodities (soybeans, grains, etc.,) are very lucrative but are subject to future imponderables—the weather (such as the recent drought), political events (such as the recent grain embargo), and potential manipulation.

Oil and gas exploration, which may have some tax shelter benefit, could make you into another J. Paul Getty, but also could cause you to file for bankruptcy. The incidence of dry holes is rapidly increasing due to the fact that the "easy" oil, for the most part, may have already been found. Note that all the aforementioned investments have been discussed without reference to the effects of inflation, which, in many cases, could wipe out the entire return.

Real Estate

Against all the above, which represent a sampling of some of the types of investments available, let us look at real estate. In terms of risk, one must consider the following:

1. *Land is an entity fixed amount*—no more is being created, and that which is close to human habitation is highly sought after.
2. *Real estate fulfills* (as far as residential property is concerned) *a basic need of mankind: shelter.*
3. *Real estate is a tangible asset*—you can actually see and feel your ownership interest. Compare this with stock, for instance. You can feel the stock certificate, but this piece of paper only represents your ownership interest. You can't feel that.
4. In the last several years, due to various factors and, in particular, tight money, *housing starts have been off considerably.* This results in even higher home prices, since demand for new housing, which has been fueled by the staggering growth in the young adult and senior citizen markets (and will be at a record level in the 1980's), exceeds the supply. This gap between supply and demand (in California alone estimates range as high as 130,000 total units annually) should continue and could actually widen in future years. This shortage of housing units results in very low vacancy rates (e.g., 1% in Los Angeles, 2% in Chicago, 1% in Miami, etc.) and, in turn, results in rental rates growing at an increasing rate. Thus, income generated from rental rates should grow rapidly in future years.
5. *Real estate,* in modern times, *has evidenced a basic continual upward trend in value,* especially in recent years and particularly in certain growth markets. Take, for example, the experience of Orange County, California. Nine years ago the median priced home sold for approximately $35,000. In 1981, that house would have sold for about $140,000, an increase of approximately $10,500 annually or an average annual rate of appreciation of about 30%. This average annual rate has shown a general increase over the years. In 1973, the average annual rate of appreciation was 17%, in 1975 it averaged 13.5%, and in 1978 the rate was up to about 21% annually. Only in a very few areas, notably those with declining employment bases, has the

overall real estate market declined in value and then often not very drastically and not for long periods of time.

6. In general, *the real estate market,* because of its breadth, diversity of ownership, and cost, *is not likely to be manipulated or completely dominated by one individual entity.*

7. *Real estate is the only area of investment not subject to the IRS's "at risk" rules.* This means that, in this area, a purchaser will be allowed deductions in excess of the amount invested ("at risk"). Thus, in real estate, there are income sheltering opportunities unavailable to other investors.

8. *Income producing real estate can be exchanged with no gain recognized and thus no taxes currently payable.* The income taxes that would have been due are deferred, possibly forever. This is not possible with many other investments.

9. *Real estate is somewhat illiquid.* This means that overnight the owner of a property could not transform that asset into dollars. But this is not something to be overly obsessed with. Liquidity will depend on the area, the specific property, and timing of the sale or other disposition. Many investments have this characteristic. This does not mean that you could not, for example, in relatively short time, arrange for an equity loan on the real estate if you need cash immediately. On the contrary, if the property has appreciated, lenders are usually anxious to loan funds.

10. If there is a foreclosure on a property, (for nonpayment of the debt), *often state legislation may prohibit or severely limit the owner's liability for a deficiency* (the debt exceeds the amount realized in the foreclosure sale). Contrast this case against other investments. If you default on your payment for stocks, for example, the stockbroker can hold you personally liable for the entire amount.

By analyzing these factors, you can see that the risk involved is relatively low compared to other forms of investment, especially when viewed in light of the significant tax benefits of ownership and disposition (as we will see), the potentially high rate of return, the effects on income, and the ability to combat inflation and use it effectively for your benefit. All of this will become clearer as you read the guide.

Probably the best commentary on the risk/reward factor comes from the action of foreign investors. Real estate in this country attracts a huge amount of foreign dollars because foreign investors feel that, dollar for dollar, the benefits vastly outweigh the risk involved. From their point of view, real estate may be the best investment, and they can purchase it in the most stable country in the world. Inflation here is minor compared to elsewhere, this country is not subject to radical political events, and prices of land and homes are very favorable compared to the remainder of the world.

When you decide to dispose of your rental property, the Tax Code again rewards you with tax benefits. On a sale of real property held more than one year and *used in the trade or business*, the gain is taxed at much more favorable capital gains rates, instead of high ordinary income rates. The maximum capital gains rate is 20% as opposed to 50% on other income. This favorable treatment is one of the tax benefits reflected in the high rate of return previously discussed. (*Note:* If there was a loss, it would be characterized as an *ordinary* loss, which means that it can directly offset ordinary income—just like your other deductions do.)

The tax difference between gain characterized as ordinary income as opposed to long-term capital gain is seen from the following:

TAX TREATMENT OF ORDINARY INCOME VS. LONG-TERM CAPITAL GAIN

	Ordinary Income	Long-Term Capital Gain
Amount of Gain[a]	$35,000 (wages)	$35,000 Long-term capital gain on sale of real property held more than one year (in this case used in a trade or business).
Amount Taxable[b]	All $35,000	Only 40% or $14,000
Marginal Rate[c]	33%	16%
Federal Income Tax[d]	$5,937	$930
Difference		**$5,007 *fewer*** tax dollars

[a]Married couple filing jointly, both under 65 years old, with two minor children living at home (4 exemptions).
[b]Each amount listed is decreased by $4,000 (for personal exemptions). No other deductions are assumed.
[c]The higher the rate, the more pronounced the difference in taxes. Assumes no other income in either case. There is a minimum tax on capital gains—this is discussed later.
[d]State tax effects have been disregarded in this calculation.

With the same amount of green dollar bills coming into your pocket, a married taxpayer filing jointly can save $5,007 in federal income tax by getting capital gains treatment instead of ordinary income treatment. The savings for a single individual (1 exemption) are even more dramatic. Instead of paying $8,772 in tax, you would only have $1,870 in tax on the capital gain—a difference of $6,902. This is one of the features of holding real property more than one year. You have effectively changed ordinary income into long-term capital gain. Just by holding the property for the right amount of time, you get a reward.

If you later refinance the property or obtain an equity loan on the property, the net loan proceeds come to you *tax-free*, and you can deduct the interest charged. In turn you are reducing your taxes. It is as if the Government is *paying you* to take the money. You can now use the additional funds to continue purchasing properties or for any purpose. You can readily see that a large net wealth is quickly established by continuing your purchases and profiting by the resulting appreciation.

If the real property is your principal residence and it is sold, special rules apply, providing certain requirements are met. In general, the gain realized on the sale of a principal residence is not recognized (and thus not presently taxed) if you replace it with another principal residence, move in within two years before or after the sale of the old residence, and the cost of the new residence is at least as much as the adjusted sales price of the old residence. Furthermore, if you are 55 years old or over, the first $125,000 of gain ($62,500 on the separate return of a married person) on the sale of your principal residence is not taxable at all. Note, however, that this is a one-time event only, and there is only one $125,000 exemption between a married couple. Note further that state tax treatment regarding this area may vary. (Calculation of gain is discussed more fully in Part IV.)

Instead of selling that piece of property you are currently renting out, why not exchange it for another suitable piece of real property? If you do this, the gain is *not recognized* at this time and thus the taxes are deferred. The rate of return (see the proforma at the end of Part II) jumps significantly to 129.55% (before effects of inflation) as opposed to 88.24% if the property were sold. Think of that— even if inflation is 10% per year (and eventually it may average this again over the long run), after a two year period you would have a net yield of *over 108%* (exchanges are discussed in detail in Part IV).

You can see, therefore, that part of the technique or method I describe is the use of the Internal Revenue Code to *help* you instead of hurting you by taking *full advantage* of what the Internal Revenue Service gives you in the real estate taxation area.

In Part I, I will discuss obtaining funds for the down payment, the loan itself, and how you can hold title to the property. In addition, qualifying for a loan will be discussed briefly.

Part I

Financing the Purchase

1

Down Payment Sources

A down payment in today's market for owner-occupied housing is typically 10 to 20% of the sales price of the property. However, for non-owner occupied housing the down payment, more than likely, will be around a 20% figure—generally not less than that. Therefore, in our $60,000 house example, a down payment of $6,000 to $12,000 might be needed if the house were purchased as a personal residence. A $12,000 down payment would probably be necessary if the house were purchased as a rental property.

Personal Assets

Raising $12,000 may not be as difficult as it initially sounds. First, you should assess your current financial position. Determine what your assets and liabilities are. You are doing what businesses do every day—establishing a balance sheet. Maybe you have some money sitting idle in a bank account, or you might have some stocks/securities that may be, given present inflation and interest rates, not very productive. You may have some assets you really do not need—for example, an extra car. You could sell these assets or use them as collateral for a loan.

Life Insurance

Inspect your life insurance policy. It very well might contain a provision permitting you to borrow on the policy at very favorable rates—4%, 6%, 8% (or less). It should not concern you greatly that there is an outstanding balance due on the loan at the time of your death because hopefully, you will have purchased assets (real property) that have appreciated significantly. The outstanding balance, and any interest that has not been repaid, will be deducted from the amount of the policy proceeds the beneficiary would have received. To provide for your beneficiary, you might instead leave one of your properties to that person. In addition, it may be a mistake to view any insurance policy as a good means to save money. It is true, it can be a forced savings plan—and if you are unable to save money any other way, then it is a *good* savings plan. However, if you are able to voluntarily save money in other ways, then a life insurance policy to serve this purpose is not very attractive, considering that it pays very low interest in terms of today's inflation and interest rates.

Relatives

Have you overlooked the obvious and most available source of funds? You may have a relative (parent, grandparent, etc.) who is willing and able to help you. This help could take the form of an interest-free loan, a very attractive low-rate loan, or an outright gift. In all of these transactions, both the relative and you have something to gain. First, let's discuss a loan. If the relative is in a high income tax bracket, he could loan you the down payment amount interest-free, since the last thing he needs is more income. If the relative has the money to lend you but needs some income, the rate you both agree on could be above that which he is currently achieving on other investments, but below that which you would otherwise have to pay.

You gain by first obtaining the money from the down payment. But, note—you are obtaining the money tax-free. In addition, the interest you do pay is tax deductible. Be aware that a loan transaction should be in writing and the loan itself payable on demand—especially if interest-free (or at a rate less than market) and between relatives. This will help establish that the loan was not a gift that could be subject to gift tax.

Speaking of gifts and the gift tax, the Economic Recovery Tax Act of 1981 has made gift taxes in many instances a thing of the past. A person can now annually give $10,000 to as many individuals as he chooses without incurring a gift tax. And a husband and wife together can make a split gift of $20,000 annually to as many persons as they choose, tax-free. (*Note:* Spouses can make unlimited gifts to each other without gift tax consequences.) If a relative gives you the down payment, he has the pleasure of assisting someone of whom he is very fond. He also gains by having the down payment amount removed from his estate. (It saves estate taxes upon his death.) In fact, if the relative gives you an appreciating asset (which you could sell to make the down payment), he will not only have the present market value removed from his estate, but also all future appreciation, although there may be gift tax consequences on any gift amounts exceeding the gift tax exclusion.

Other private individuals can also be good sources of funds for both the down payment and loan financing, and similar rules apply.

Refinancing/Equity Loans

Maybe you already own some real property, either commercial, industrial, or residential, or even a business in which a considerable equity base has been established. Leaving that equity in the property or business is, in effect, wasting a very valuable asset. Use the equity to obtain the down payment amount. Normally, a financial institution should allow you to either refinance or take out an equity loan. Refinancing is just as it sounds—an entirely new loan for, say, 80% of the current value is made—at present interest rates. (The old loan is retired.) An equity loan is a little different in that the financial institution, without disturbing the existing loan, is lending you up to 80% of current value of your real property (less the amount of the existing debt). The attractiveness of this financing source depends, in part, on the level of current interest rates. Note that an equity loan will typically be several percentage points above the current rate available in connection with loans evidenced by first trust deeds/mortgages. However, you should not become overly conscious of these higher rates since the interest you will pay is deductible. Therefore, the cost of these funds can be considerably reduced. For example, for a person in the 50% tax bracket with additional monthly interest payments of $100 due to one of the aforementioned sources, the real cost is only ½ that amount, or $50. (More on this subject in Chapter 26.)

Federal Programs

Even if you do not presently own your own home, various government programs may be available to you. The fact is that you may not need *any* cash down payment at all, or at the least it may be very small. (*Note:* I will discuss these programs at this point in the guide, although they also apply under the loan financing chapters of this Part.)

VA Loans

The GI Bill is available to veterans who served at least 90 days between September 16, 1940, and January 31, 1955, or at least 181 days of active service since the latter date (with an honorable discharge), or those veterans with 181 days active service since the latter date who are still on active duty.

In this program there is the possibility that *no* down payment will be required. Lenders may participate in 100% financing since the Veterans Administration is willing to guarantee a part of the loan (up to the entitlement amount which varies with the individual). This guarantee makes the lender's position more secure in the event of a loss. The veteran must obtain a certificate of eligibility from the Veterans Administration. The entitlement can be used over and over again, providing that the GI loan is paid off at the time of sale of the property. Note that the entitlement amount is *not* the maximum GI loan that can be granted. Instead, the entitlement is the amount of the lender's guarantee, and this influences his willingness to make the loan. Be aware that this program can only be utilized to purchase property used as your principal residence.

Additional beneficial features of the VA loan program include:

1. Statutory interest rates (varying with the market) which are relatively low in comparison to other loan sources.
2. The term of the loan can be up to 30 years.
3. Points (charges of interest in advance for use of the money) are charged to the seller. The borrower is prohibited from paying these and, thus, the seller is subsidizing the buyer's financing, even if the sales price has been increased to reflect these costs (But, note: the lender can charge the buyer a loan fee of 1% of the loan).

4. The VA inspects the properties involved to insure compliance with building standards (but do not equate this inspection and approval as a "guarantee" of structural soundness and quality).

FHA Loans

The Federal Housing Administration loan program is another government program that can be of importance to all U.S. residents in that the down payment and interest rate may be considerably less than with conventional financing. The FHA does not lend funds directly. Instead, it works like the VA program in that it reduces for the lender the risk of potential loss on default. The mechanics are different, however; the FHA provides mortgage insurance as opposed to guaranteeing part of the loan. (This insurance will cost the borrower ½% in interest.) The effect is the same and many of the same benefits are available, although the maximum loan amount is $67,500 for a single family residence (however, in certain areas such as Los Angeles, the maximum is $90,000), contrasted to a potential 100% financed VA deal. The down payment in an FHA situation will be 3% of the first $25,000 of appraised value; 20% on the balance; and 100% on the excess of selling price over appraised value. Additionally, a veteran may have enhanced FHA benefits in several of their programs.

State Programs

Various state programs may assist you. For example, in California, the state finances a program for assisting California veterans in buying homes/farms (the Cal-Vet program). The state puts up the money to complete a purchase and takes title to the property (even though the veteran has put up some of the money). Interest rates are extremely low (although variable) and, effectively, the purchaser contributes at least 3% of the appraised value (land and building) as a down payment.

There are several snags in this program to be aware of:

1. Application to the Cal-Vet program will involve significant time delays in consideration of a loan (now about 6 months—especially for the most recent eligible veterans)

and often the Cal-Vet funds are exhausted prematurely in any particular year (since only a certain dollar amount of revenue bonds are sold at any one time to finance the program).

2. The maximum home loan amount is only $55,000.

3. The veteran must apply within 25 years following release from active service (unless disabled due to that active service, or a prisoner of war).

4. The program is not available to veterans serving between February 1, 1955, and August 4, 1964, and since May 7, 1975.

5. The property must be used as a residence.

The combination of these requirements, especially in today's world of high residence prices, makes it difficult, but not impossible to use this program.

Another current program can be found in Alaska. This state provides a subsidized mortgage program administered by the Alaska Housing Finance Corp. which allows its participants to make only a minimal down payment (5%) on a home. Interest rates range from 6% for low-income residents to 10% for all others except veterans (9%). Through a combination of bond revenues and state appropriations, a home buyer can borrow up to $147,000 for a single family home and $189,000 for a duplex.

Other government programs may be worth seeking. For instance, the California National Guard, through the issuance of revenue bonds, recently began a home finance program for Guard members. Loans will be granted up to $55,000 for 30 years at 11% (as compared to 14 to 16% mortgage rates as of this writing). The loan amount can be up to 95% of the purchase price. Thus, a Guard member could purchase a house worth nearly $57,900 with only 5% (or about $2,900) down, provided that he occupies that house. Cities (Los Angeles, for example) are now utilizing this same technique to aid their residents.

Other Methods

As you may have realized already, the easiest way to raise a down payment is not having to raise it at all. In many instances, a house can be purchased with minimal or no cash outlay. You will have to be creative in your approach. Mortgage insurance for example. Talk to your lender and find out if he will provide 90% or higher financing (instead of approximately 80%) in return for your purchase of mortgage insurance. This may increase your monthly payments, but some of this additional expense is deductible, the amount depending, in part, on how you characterize your purchases. If this is a house you will rent out, and you treat your activity as a true "trade or business," mortgage insurance may be a legitimate business expense (and of course, the additional interest is deductible).

Wraparound Mortgages

Or, you and the seller can agree to a wraparound transaction (discussed at length later in this Part) where he will in effect finance his equity in the house by taking back an all-inclusive trust deed/wraparound mortgage for the entire or most of the purchase price. In this way, you will have large monthly payments, but minimal down payment. Similarly, you might get the seller to take back a second mortgage for *part* of the price.

Seller-Paid Closing Costs

You could reduce your initial cash outlay if you can convince the seller to pay your closing costs. He might, because he will not have to put up cash—the funds will be deducted in escrow from the amount he will receive. The seller could assign a balance in his impound account to the buyer. Similarly, he could assign a paid-up fire insurance policy. Note that if you wish to use these last few techniques, the lender should be consulted beforehand. It must be understood that a loan agreement is conditioned on the fact that the purchaser-borrower will have a certain equity in the transaction (down payment plus closing costs). The lender wants this equity amount to be as large as possible to give him added security in case of a default. If the seller pays some of your closing costs, your equity is reduced. This may cause the lender to withdraw or lower the amount of the loan, unless he has agreed to these changes in the normal closing process. Of course, if a VA loan is involved, there may not be any problem, since you may not have to actually *pay* any down payment or loan costs at all (although you could be *assessed* some costs).

Real Estate Syndicates

To reduce your down payment and initial costs, why not consider buying a property together with others in a common ownership situation. A venture such as this is called a *real estate syndicate*—a group of investors who have pooled their funds for the purpose of owning property. Most of these syndicates are taxable as partnerships or as corporations unless an election is made to be treated as a Real Estate Investment Trust, which will be discussed later. In fact, generally speaking, the common ownership of income-producing real property results in the automatic formation of a partnership for federal income tax purposes.

Advantages. The vast majority of these syndicates take the form of a limited partnership with the organizer acting as a general or managing partner. The general partner has unlimited liability, whereas the limited partners are liable only up to the amount of capital contributed. The partnership itself files an information return with the Internal Revenue Service, but pays no income taxes. The income and deductions on the property are "passed through" to the partners in proportion to their interest, and are reported by each on his own respective income tax return. The partnership, in its agreement, can indicate a different allocation of profit and losses, and it will probably be followed by the Internal Revenue Service, as long as the principal purpose is not to avoid taxes. If there are substantial economic effects (basically where you have given up something to get something in return) not involving tax consequences, the allocation will be permitted.

However, the IRS does require that a partner's share of annual cash flow equal his share of taxable income/loss. Gain/loss is reported by each partner in the year in which the partnership year ends. For example, if there was a gain in the fiscal year ending February 28, 1984, but the partner's year ends on December 31, 1983, the gain is reported for the 1984 year. *However,* the partners will have the use of their shares of this gain tax-free until April 15, 1985, when a tax will be owing.

The syndicator (or organizer) must disclose an immense amount of information about himself, the project, financial information, etc. In addition, the offering may be required to be registered with the Securities and Exchange Commission or a state agency (or be required to qualify for a state permit). The process is very time-consuming and costly. However, private offerings are exempt from both SEC and state registration, providing they meet certain federal and state requirements.

What are the additional advantages of a limited partnership syndicate over other forms of common ownership? Besides making it easier to raise initial funds, and the tax consequences, more financing can be obtained in this manner, and an otherwise temporarily uneconomic investment could possibly carry itself where in different circumstances it would not. In addition, there is one managing person who speaks for the entire group, instead of a myriad of voices speaking at once. Thus, assuming a good managing partner is chosen, management should be easier, clearer, and more economical. If you are the organizer, you can receive management fees, commissions from sales, and other further financial remuneration.

One other benefit of holding the property in partnership name (and calling the partnership by the street address or similar name) is that activation of the due-on-sale clause (discussed later) in the mortgage (which mandates that the lender is paid off in full upon sale of the property or other events) may be avoided upon resale of the property to others. You would be selling your interests in the *partnership* to others and not the property itself. Since no title has changed hands, the clause is not activated and the purchaser gets the benefit of a lower-interest loan. And, in effect, you have been able to sell the property and go on to something else. To ensure this result, a lawyer should be consulted for his expertise in preparing documents and in interpretating the due-on-sale clause prior to the sale of your interests.

Disadvantages. What are the disadvantages? In any partnership or group situation, you lose the control you otherwise would have had if you entered the venture alone. Second, a poorly drafted partnership agreement could cause the partnership to be taxed as a corporation, with its double taxation—first at the income level, then at the dividend level (*and* with no "pass through" of income and deductions.) Third, the mere fact that the partnership exists has several implications. One is that a separate income tax return (information only) must be filed each year. Another is that the property is owned by the partnership, not the partners. This has an effect when one of the partners dies: since only the partnership interest (and not the property) is includable in your estate, this results in lower estate taxes; but, at the same time, only your partnership interest and not the property, receives an upward basis adjustment for its fair market value. Also, since only the property and not the partnership interest is depreciable, the beneficiary of your interest may find that he could have been entitled to a larger depreciation deduction if the property itself had been owned directly by the partners, including the descendent, as tenants in common.

The partnership entity could be a very good vehicle to provide a possible tax-free college fund for your children. Take this case: you find a property you wish to purchase for use as a rental unit. Instead of establishing one partnership that would own the entire property, set up *two* partnerships—one that owns the land and one that owns the building. The children are the partners in the former partnership, and the parents are the partners in the latter.

Each parent could have previously made $10,000 gifts to each of the children, or $20,000 jointly, which they will apply to the purchase price of the land. Remember, anyone can make a gift of $10,000 or less each year to as many persons as he wishes without incurring gift tax. If necessary, the children can borrow the remaining funds to be paid for the land from their parents, and any interest paid by the children is a deductible expense for them. The parents would pay the children rent for the land lease. This represents income to the children and a deductible business expense for the parents (if the building is used in a trade or business). Since the children are in very low or no income brackets at all, taxes to the children are minimal. The children have cash flow and the parents have tax shelter (from the depreciation on the building).

Just because you own property with others *does not* mean that you cannot avoid treatment as a partnership entity. To insure the common owners' right to be treated as individual owners of individual interest in the property, they should file a dummy partnership return in the first year of ownership, specifically electing not to be treated as a partnership for tax purposes.

2

Down Payment Alternatives

Alternative methods exist to diminish the size of your down payment. Some are more significant than others but all should be investigated.

Shared Equity Purchase Programs (SEP)

This is a variation on the group purchase of real estate property. In a previous discussion, limited partnership ownership of a property was discussed. In Chapter 6, ownership as tenants in common and joint tenancy are explained. Usually, in each of these cases, the partner or common or joint tenant would contribute his share to the down payment and further to the ongoing costs of ownership, including mortgage costs, taxes, insurance, etc. At the sale, each person would then receive his proportionate amount of the appreciation.

In the shared equity programs, an investor or relative contributes all or part of the down payment in return for a specified agreed upon percentage of the appreciation upon sale. The investor/relative does not contribute to any other expenses. Payment of these expenses is the sole responsibility of the noninvestor/relative party. However, the larger the down payment, the smaller the monthly expenses should be.

These programs, which in effect are types of joint ventures, are becoming increasingly popular. In some cases, parents are taking out second trust deeds on their homes to finance a down payment for one of their children. Some builders and other investors are offering programs where the qualified owner-occupant will be provided one-half of the down payment in exchange for one-half of the appreciation. Although the builder/investor co-signs the first trust deed loan, the owner-occupant is responsible for loan payments, taxes, insurance, utilities, repairs, and maintenance.

Even the government sector has recognized this as a good vehicle to get people into housing, especially young families/households and, at the same time, obtain an excellent return. For example, California and other states are considering various pilot programs. The state will provide money for the down payment. Upon sale, refinancing, or purchase by the owner/occupant of the government's interest, the state will share in any of the profits.

Of course, a business agreement in this instance is essential— especially when dealing with family relationships. These relationships often become sticky. It is far better to have all rights and duties stipulated in advance than to be surprised later. You would do this in any other business deal with a stranger. Take it from me, make the agreement and do it in writing. I would be remiss in my duties as a lawyer if I didn't mention several key items and contingencies that the agreement should cover. (Some common answers have been provided.)

1. *Default of the occupant.* What happens when the occupant decides he is tired of making the monthly mortgage payment, etc.?

2. *Who is responsible for ordinary maintenance of the real property?* Generally, the occupant should pay for these costs.

3. *Who is responsible for major improvements to the property?* For example, if the property requires an entirely new plumbing system, who pays for it? Of course, a wide range of possible sharing formulas exist but, generally, use of the same percentage as that prescribed for sharing of appreciation would be reasonable.

4. *Whose consent is necessary to make these major improvements and what is the result of an improvement made without this consent?* Often, both parties must agree. Thus, if the

occupant makes a repair without this consent, he must bear the entire cost.

5. *What happens upon death of a party?*
6. *What happens upon bankruptcy of a party?*
7. *What happens upon a withdrawal from the "joint venture"?*
8. *What percentage of the appreciation will each party receive?* What events trigger this split (sale, refinancing, etc.)? Is this percentage applicable to all appreciation, or only after the return of the parties' respective original contributions to the venture?

If you provide a legal description of the property in this agreement (and you should), you can and should record the document with the County Recorder. This represents added protection to you.

Often parties also split expenses in these shared equity programs. For example, one company making these SEP's pays 75% of the down payment, 50% of the closing costs, and later obtains 50% of the appreciation, after original contributions are deducted. However, both the company and the occupant each pay 50% of the mortgage payments, insurance costs, and real estate taxes. In this plan, the occupant would pay a monthly rental to the company to cover the company's share of mortgage costs plus a reasonable return on its investment.

Another form of SEP may be to your liking. In this case, the parties would still split equally the monthly payments, but each would receive an agreed upon cumulative return on his total investment, except for the monthly payments paid by the occupant. So the investor, upon a sale, would get a fixed cumulative rate of return on his down payment plus on the total of his half of the monthly payment. The occupant would be entitled to the same rate of return but only on his down payment. Out of the equity, the investor and occupant would get their respective original investments back, plus their respective rates of return. Any remaining excess would be split equally.

This form has advantages for the occupant in that his monthly payments are much less than they would be, as is his down payment, and yet he has no current out-of-pocket cost for these benefits. Upon sale, the accounts are rectified as described previously. This also means that it should be easier for the occupant to qualify.

Note that the Shared Appreciation Mortgage (SAM) is closely allied to discussion of the SEP. However, because of its advantages primarily in the reduction of interest rates and, thus, monthly payments, I will discuss it at a later time.

These shared equity purchase plans have some unresolved questions. First, there is the possibility that in some states, such as California, a transfer of a party's interest to another would trigger a property reappraisal. This, in turn would result in significantly higher property taxes in many cases. Second, the vacation home rules may apply (Section 280A of the Internal Revenue Code).

Notwithstanding the aforementioned questions, the shared equity purchase plans have obvious merit and, in the future, will provide a tremendous help to buyers of real property. Investors also do well, getting an excellent return plus tax advantages of depreciation and the insurance write-off, aside from their part of the deductions for taxes and interest.

The Seller as Co-Investor

If you are short of the required down payment and the seller doesn't want to carry the difference back, use the limited partnership vehicle discussed previously. You and the seller will be partners. The seller will be a limited partner. For example, assume that on a $60,000 house, the seller seeks a 25% down payment ($15,000). You only have $10,000. The seller then takes back $5,000 in equity, becoming a $5,000/$15,000 or 33⅓% limited partner. You don't own the entire building, only 67⅔%, but you would have *no* interest in the building otherwise.

Land Leases

In an ordinary situation, if you were buying a $60,000 house in Main Town, USA, you would be buying both the house and the land it sits on. In a land-lease deal, as is common in Hawaii, you are buying the building, but *leasing* the land underneath.

This aids you, the buyer, in two ways. First, since the land price is not included in the deal, the cost of the deal is reduced, as is the down payment. Second, since you are only buying the improvements, your mortgage payment is reduced. Of course, the lease payment for the land is to be included in your monthly costs, but experience has shown the lease payment to be relatively small and fixed in many cases for at least the first 10 to 15 years. It rises significantly after that with additional long-term periods of stability in payment amounts. So overall, your monthly expenditures could be less.

Additionally, you have the option to buy the land at specific prices over the term of the lease. This represents a valuable right, although due to the rent subsidization, it appears that you probably would not exercise that right. (If you exercised the right, you would get a parcel of land for less than market value but give up many years of rent subsidies. Thus, your opportunity cost is too high.)

The potential problem with this arrangement is in the possible nondeductibility of the lease payment. Ordinarily, lease payments are not deductible and,thus, this hurts your tax saving efforts. On the other hand, mortgage interest is and a mortgage payment (interest part) is a tax-saving device. However, lease payments might be deductible if the lease term is more than 30 years, which is often the case in land leases. This treatment is possible because the IRS considers a lease of this term the equivalent of ownership.

Distress Situations

The Builders' Dilemma

Many builders/developers are finding themselves in a very precarious situation. They have a great deal of unsold inventory, with a tremendous carrying cost in terms of high construction interest rates, while the number of available qualified buyers is dwindling and mortgage rates are peaking. The question becomes whether to sell now or go broke later. To alleviate their tight financial circumstances, they are in some cases auctioning off their developments to the highest bidder. While winning bids have generally been in excess of the minimum bid asked, they have usually been below the market price of similar homes—often significantly less.

Another device being used widely by builders and developers is the buy-down. There are two common methods of builder buy-downs. The first is the ordinary form used and reduces the buyer's monthly payments. This method will be discussed in the section entitled "The 'New' Mortgages" in Chapter 3 of this Part. The second method involves a determination by the builder of the amount it would cost him to "buy-down" the current interest rates to an interest rate that will attract buyers and allow the properties to sell. He then gives this amount in a lump sum to the buyer. Thus, the buyer could use this amount as part of the down payment. Note, the interest rate would be the high current rate. Thus, this form of the buy-down would only appeal to buyers with incomes to qualify for the loan but who are short on a cash down payment. Also, be aware that in many cases, the builder actually may have raised his price to include his cost of the buy-down. This obviously would tend to reduce the beneficial effects of this device to the buyer.

The Uncooperative Tenant

You have heard the expression a hundred times— "We all make mistakes." This is your opportunity to capitalize on someone else's. That is, selecting a tenant is an art and once in a while a bad one is chosen. It is much easier to make a mistake if a landlord/owner does not heed the advice given in Part 2. Be that as it may, some owners of single-family houses have bums for tenants. They're destroyers or sloppy and, on top of it, are never home, or if they are home, will not let any potential buyer see the place. Real estate agents become alienated. In short, the owner wants to sell badly and can't.

It is going to take a critical eye to look at the house beyond the mess or the dirt. Remember, if the building is basically sound but has cosmetic defects, you will submit a discounted offer and more than likely it, or something close to it, will be accepted. Your job in finding these properties has been made much easier recently, at least in some areas. For example, recent court cases have let several local real estate boards make the multiple listing books available to the public for a fee. These books include all properties that have been listed by brokers willing to split a commission with another broker if that broker should sell the property. Many lists are very detailed, or you can do the obvious and ask real estate brokers about for sale rental properties that are "hard to show." The advantage of this type of purchase is a lower price (under the market) for a good solid unit. This, in turn, reflects a low down payment and a smaller mortgage. In fact, the owner may be so anxious to sell, he may be willing to carry a second mortgage on the property at a favorable rate to you.

One major problem area: You bought the building, not the

tenant. Your deal should be structured whereby the seller must get rid of the tenant *prior* to closing. Don't buy the headache, but learn from it and profit from it.

Divorce

I feel bad talking about this one—really. I hate to see this happen, but it does and life goes on. Again, it is a mistake made by someone (or two people). By combing through public records, legal records, and legal publications (which your attorney can suggest) you can discover a wealth of information on recent divorces, the property owned jointly by the couple, and their addresses. This obviously takes time and should be considered primarily for that reason. Most people will not do this amount of work to save some money. We are all naturally lazy. The more aggressive and ambitious of the population will thus study the aforementioned records and find potential sellers.

The court decree will often stipulate that the house is to be sold in order to provide funds for a property distribution. And, many times, there is a time limit. You be the one at the right time and place with a discounted offer.

For Sale by Owner

This is a favorite for many investors. They seek these out first because they are much easier to find. For sale by owner ads and signs are simple to monitor. So with this "for sale by owner" group you must move fast to talk to these sellers.

The key reason these sellers are vulnerable is that they lack the experience and knowledge of the marketplace. Often, they have a less than adequate understanding of comparable sales and market values in their area. Thus, they are likely to price their property over or under the current market value. You may be able to capitalize on one that is underpriced or even on an overpriced property (submitting a low offer) because the seller needs a quick sale. He may be more apt to accept a lower offer since he has no broker commission to pay, which often amounts to 6% of the purchase price.

Owner Lives Outside the State

An owner who lives away from the area in which he has invested in real property eventually will not have a true handle on market value for his property unless he has researched the market or has sought some expert advice. Many probably never should have bought the property, since they weren't aware of proper managerial techniques or just did a bad job at managing the property. This person may be extremely anxious to sell and will accept the first *reasonable* offer.

The assessor will necessarily send the tax bill to the owner's out of state address. Therefore, if you review the tax lists of these people, you will find them. Write or call and make then an offer (a low one of course).

A House Long on the Market

Sometimes a property is on the market for longer than the average time period. There is a reason for this, although it is often a superficial circumstance or event that is the cause. For example, the tenant has not kept the interior of the house clean and the house shows badly. Or the tenant requires an appointment in advance for the agent to show the house. Or the house needs some cosmetic repair such as coat of paint or new carpeting.

It could be that the house is vacant and the owner has been transferred to another city. He is carrying two mortgages and has to sell. In this or any of the above cases, a low offer may turn the trick.

Don't Just Sit on Your Real Estate License

If you have a license and are engaged in the sale of real estate on a regular basis, skip this section. If not and you either do not possess a license in your area or don't use it, you can save some money by doing the following. Since sales commissions (often 6%) are split between listing broker, listing agent, selling agent, and selling broker, why not act as the selling agent and (if you possess the broker's license) the selling broker?

You will receive half of the commission (3% of the purchase price). Assume you have a $60,000 sale that requires a 20% down payment ($12,000). This 3% commission amounts to $1,800. But, in regard to the down payment, you now need to raise only an additional $10,200 (the original requirement of $12,000 less the $1,800 cash commission received). Thus, 15% of your immediate cash needs to purchase the house has been eliminated.

Since you are now the seller's agent, you must bear in mind, all of those good things your real estate teachers told you when you were studying for your license: disclosure, disclosure, disclosure. You have an obligation to disclose completely, fully, and fairly all material facts. To do otherwise is bad play but, worse yet, subjects you to an ever-widening professional liability area.

You face very little chance of being categorized a "dealer" for purposes of the IRS just because you act as the selling agent. As described in a later section, the IRS looks at a long list of circumstances and events in which the investor engages. (See Chapter 30, Part IV for a number of points of which to be aware with respect to determining whether your activity is more like an investor or a dealer.

Look for a Smaller House

This is not as obvious a suggestion as it sounds. Of course, buying a smaller house generally will mean a lower price than a larger house, and thus a lower down payment. But what makes this a reasonable alternative is that the typical household in America is getting smaller. In fact, in 1960 the average household size was 3.37 persons. By 1980, it had dropped to 2.72 persons. At the same time, the number of households is increasing. Therefore, there is going to be a much greater market demand for smaller housing units as the decade progresses. Note that this is just the opposite trend from previous decades. In 1980, the average house size approximated 1,700 square feet. By 1990, the average size of a house should approach 1,500 square feet, a reduction of 11.8%, making your smaller house more attractive as time passes. Homes as small as 600 to 700 square feet are being built today in some parts of the country.

The No-Money-Down Purchase

Recently, various individuals have been promoting the efficacy of no-money-down real property purchases. They give seminars and write books on the subject. Deals about which they speak are done every day. And I know that they earn as much or more from their seminars and books as they do from their own real estate activities. If you are really interested, their books and seminars are informative.

However, before I briefly mention some of their techniques, let me submit a few considerations to you. First, the average seller is interested in a cold cash down payment. Period. He doesn't know you or your record. What if you are a fraud? Then the seller is stuck with a worthless promise to pay.

Second, the person who doesn't want cash in a lump sum but prefers a steady income stream must first be found. That requires a tremendous investment of your time. If you are like me, your other activities already occupy the bulk of your time. And, since time costs money, this expense must be added to any no-money-down deal you do arrange. Since the program I outline in this guide refers to growth areas (which will probably be outside of your own home town area), looking for these deals just isn't practical.

Third, your real estate contacts cannot come close to those of the renowned speakers in the no-money-down area. They have been in the business for years and have the experience in this field. Even they will tell you that the same person seldom closes this type of deal repeatedly. Once in a while, maybe. And, I would venture to say that a person in the business will find these properties because of his experience before the property ever hits the (street) market. And, as one proponent of a no-money-down deal recently discovered, not all of them are great financial successes just because they did not require any funds as a down payment.

The proponents of such deals rely extensively on the following techniques as well as others:

1. Pre-sale refinancing by the seller to permit the seller to receive the cash he needs.

2. Contracts of sale, where title is not passed until the contract conditions are met (for protection to the seller).

3. Promissory notes, including personal IOUs.

4. Second and third mortgages (and a commensurate rise in the price of the property).

5. Spending time with the seller to assess his noncash needs and meeting these needs.

6. "Balloon" down payments (or installment down payments by the buyer).

7. Deferral of payment of the down payment for a specific period (e.g., six months) with no initial mortgage payments.

These techniques do work. But remember, the seller has to accept these terms for a deal to be cut. Again, not that many sellers are motivated to sell by these techniques. If you can arrange a no-money-down deal, more power to you. You have the best of all worlds. However, my experience has been that in the fast-paced real estate world, especially in terms of out-of-state investment, looking for a deal with a *reasonable* down payment (assuming all other factors are equal) can be as cost-effective in the long run with much less hassle.

3

Loan Financing Sources

Assuming you have raised the funds for the down payment and other associated sales costs, you must now find loan financing and qualify for that loan. If your are buying a house to use as a rental unit, it will be slightly more difficult than if you were buying for your own personal use. This occurs for two primary reasons. First, lenders want as much security as possible. That is, they wish to be certain that the property will be worth at least the loan amount should they need to foreclose or you want to sell the property later. Their reasoning includes the thought that an owner-occupier will generally not harm the property and generally will take better care of the property than a renter. Second, many areas of the country have been overrun with true speculators and quick-buck artists who buy and sell properties very rapidly to drive up the price of properties to artificially high levels, thus reaping large gains for the rapid appreciation of the properties. Lenders are rightfully wary of these types and wish to curtail their activity, since it is very disruptive in the marketplace. The same reasoning in part is responsible for a higher down payment requirement for non-owner occupied housing. Remember, your intent is not to speculate but to reduce your tax liability by operating rental units as your "trade or business" and, in turn, providing places for people to live. Careful cooperation with a lender will be necessary so as to allay his rightful concerns.

There are many sources of loan financing which will be detailed

LIFE INSURANCE COMPANIES   25

below. However, you should be aware that both within a specified loan source category, and among all the categories together, the interest rate, other charges, requirements, and availability of funds differ and may differ significantly.

Savings and Loan Associations

These entities were established for the primary purpose of providing a safe place for savings and to lend money on a long-term basis for housing. They are the largest single source of residential loan financing. Recently, operating rules for these associations have been modified to permit longer terms (up to 40 years) and lower down payments (10%) on *some* home loans.

Commercial Banks

Banks represent the second largest source of long-term financing, although they finance a wide diversity of loans.

Mutual Savings Banks

Although unknown to many parts of the country (they operate primarily in the Middle Atlantic and New England regions of the country), they represent the third largest source of residential long-term financing. These banks specialize in making loans for single family housing. *Note:* The term *mutual* in the name signifies that the bank is owned by the depositors, similar to a federally chartered savings and loan association. Even though these banks may not exist in certain parts of the country, they may be important, since money may reach those states such as California through the use of mortgage loan correspondents (also known as mortgage bankers). These people find mortgage borrowers and match their needs with entities (lenders) such as mutual savings banks, life insurance companies, pension funds, and trusts with money to lend.

Life Insurance Companies

Life insurance companies play a major role in financing residential real estate. They represent the last of the "big four" lenders in this field. Typically, life insurance companies utilize mortgage loan correspondents (mortgage bankers) in arranging loans.

Other Sources

In the aggregate, the following potential lenders comprise a significant portion of the residential loan market. However, I have them in *alphabetical* order and *not* order of importance, since any *one* of these sources does not nearly have the impact that any of the "big four" do at this time.

Credit Unions

A credit union is a form of a cooperative savings and loan society united by a common interest (such as common employment, membership in a labor union, etc.). The members purchase shares—the equivalent to making a deposit in a financial institution such as a savings and loan. These members, and only these members, can borrow money. Some of these loans are made to finance real estate. Note, however, that state and federal loan term limits as well as potentially high interest rates compared to other sources, may make this source somewhat less attractive. However, you may still want to obtain *some* of the needed funds in this manner.

Finance Companies

Generally, most people think of these as companies with money to help them to consolidate debts or purchase other items. They usually operate in the high-risk segment of the financing market. But, many of these companies have been attracted to making real estate loans because of the security they offer them. You probably would only go to this source if you could not qualify for a loan at a bank/savings and loan or if you had not adequately checked out other sources of financing. The total interest rates are high, but other fees (loan processing, etc.) may be minimal, so that their rate may be almost equivalent to other sources. However, the maximum amount of the loan may be quite low and the maximum term of the loan quite short.

Individuals

Private individuals like to make first mortgage/trust deed loans because of their attractive rate of return. (They may also be interested in making second mortgage/trust deed loan financing.) The important factor to note here is the freedom from Government regulation. You will be able to clearly negotiate the terms of the loan. You will be able to negotiate loan expenses. You should make it clear to other people either by conversation, advertisement, or otherwise that you are seeking these funds from private investors. This could be quite a beneficial source of funds for you.

Mortgage Bankers/Mortgage Companies

Mortgage bankers act as middlemen who raise funds from various sources on the one hand, and locate borrowers for those funds on the other. They are not limited to one source of funds, but have access to many—and they have the knowledge of where the money is available. These entities actively seek to make real estate loans and might be contacted.

Mortgage Loan Brokers

This is a different entity than the aforementioned mortgage banker. A mortgage broker, for a fee, can set up a specific first, second, or third mortgage. He does this by matching potential lenders with potential borrowers. His *primary* function is to help the borrower make up the gap between the amount of the first loan and the total loan amount necessary. Various state laws have an impact on terms and type of this activity, but this is another area which could be of potential benefit to you.

Pension Funds

Both the Government and trade unions have expressed a great deal of interest in investing pension money into home mortgages. Two states, Texas and Massachusetts, have begun to channel $20 million each into residential mortgage markets, and six more states are considering this approach. However, this represents only a minis-cule amount compared to the $160 billion in state pension money available. Thus, this could be a very dynamic source of funds in the future.

Trade unions want to enter the field for several reasons:

1. To finance secure loans that provide good returns.
2. To spur construction and thus raise employment levels for their members.
3. To increase contribution to the plans which is the result of the additional construction activity.

These funds can offer their participants loans at below market rate if the risk warrants it. However, many of these trade unions propose to lend funds to the general public in addition to their members. Again, this source would be a bonanza to borrowers due to the sheer size of the pension fund totals.

Real Estate Investment Trusts and Syndicates

These entities were discussed in the first part of this chapter in terms of their ability to buy and own real property. However, they can also make real estate loans. For the most part, these entities will have too much staff, costs, etc., to make a real estate loan on a single-family residence feasible from a profit standpoint. But you can try.

4

Types of Loans

Conventional Mortgages

For about 50 years, the only real game in town with regard to residential loan financing revolved around the conventional or fixed interest rate mortgage (or trust deed).* Generally, the term has been 30 years. For many years, this type of loan provided stability and security to both the lender and borrower. The lender was willing to loan money on this basis in times of moderate to low inflation for several reasons. First, he had a quantifiable, locked-in rate. Second, he generally had a spread of up to several points between the rate he was charging and the rate he was paying for his funds. (The inflation rate was also up to several points less than the interest rate he was charging.) Third, in better economies, people would move from house to house relatively frequently. Since these mortgages included prepayment penalty and due-on-sale clauses (discussed later in this chapter) and since the lender obtained fees for loan origination from the writing of new loans, the lender earned significant income in this process. Additionally, his loan portfolio yield would continually be updated and reflect a relatively consistent rate spread.

---

*Note: Throughout this guide *mortgage* and *trust deed* will be used interchangeably.

Advantages to Borrowers

The borrower would want to make this type of loan since he would have a stable monthly payment around which he could plan his budget. Second, he would be paying off the loan with increasingly cheaper dollars, as inflation continues. The lender would bear the entire interest rate and inflation rate risk. Third, the borrower's principal balance would be reduced (amortized) over time. Thus, at the end of the term of the loan, he would own the property free and clear of any encumbrances.

Disadvantages to Lenders

Recently, lenders have been reluctant to make a fixed-rate loan for several reasons. Inflation has been at very high levels and the economic climate has been very unstable. Thus, the lender found that the cost of money exceeded what he could charge for this type of loan. Lenders found that they held a great number of old loans at low rates in their portfolios, since people were not moving anymore. At the same time, the lender, due to Government regulations and interest rate limitations, could not attract the savings that provide the basis for residential mortgages. In effect, the lender realized that he was bearing the entire interest and inflation rate risk and it was killing him. The fixed-rate loans that have been available carry such high rates that borrowers can't qualify for the loans. In addition, the due-on-sale clause, the lender's last defense mechanism to obtain a better yield from his loan portfolio, has been under savage attack.

The Due-on-Sale Clause

The due-on-sale clause stipulates that if the owner of the property sells, conveys, or otherwise alienates the property, or any part thereof, then the entire loan balance is immediately due and payable. At least in the case of state chartered banks and savings and loans in California (and possibly other states), this clause is no longer automatically enforceable. The institution must go further to determine if the security would be impaired or a greater risk of default exists if the new purchaser were to take over the loan payments. If not, the purchaser is to be allowed to assume the present loan.

The rule as it pertains to federally chartered savings and loans is now settled, after a long series of court challenges. Formerly (as of June 8, 1976), the rule in the 9th Circuit (Arizona, California, Idaho, Montana, Nevada, Oregon, Washington, Alaska, Hawaii, and Guam) was that the clause was automatically enforceable and the area was governed by the Federal Home Loan Bank Board. Recent rulings at the Appellate Court and Supreme Court levels in California made this clause unenforceable or enforceable depending on whose side you were on in the transaction. In July 1981, five cases were decided by the Appellate Courts—the gist was that the federally chartered savings and loans were governed by the state law of real property and mortgages in which they do business. Thus, the federally chartered savings and loans would be unable to automatically enforce these clauses. This was the precedent until June 28, 1982.

In late August, 1981, another Appellate Court ruled that the federally chartered institutions are not governed by state law and, therefore, they can automatically enforce the clause. However, this did not become law since the California Supreme Court acted to render the opinion decertified. On June 28, 1982, the U.S. Supreme Court decided that regulations passed by the Federal Home Loan Bank Board, allowing federally chartered savings and loans to automatically enforce due-on-sale clauses, take precedence over the California Supreme Court 1978 *Wellenkamp* decision. Thus, in summary, at least in the case of federally chartered savings and loans, automatic enforcement of the clause will be permitted. It should be noted that it is very likely that state chartered institutions will switch to federal charters, or legislation (federal and/or state) will be passed so as to provide the state institutions with this same enforcement power. Federally chartered banks probably will also have this power.

Any present owner of a property with a low fixed-rate mortgage on it obviously would want the due-on-sale clause to be unenforceable and the loan assumable by a buyer of his property since the property becomes much more saleable. However, with regard to new mortgages, if lenders are not permitted to enforce a due-on-sale clause (in a fixed-rate loan) and upgrade their portfolios, all consumers will be hurt in the long run since few lenders are going to loan money at fixed rates at times when the cost of funds exceeds the rate earned, and when interest rates are skyrocketing. Any available fixed-rate loans will be at extremely high rates and, most likely, only 1 to 3% of buyers could qualify. Nothing could have caused the doom of the fixed-rate mortgage quicker than the unenforceability issue.

The fixed-rate mortgage has not, at this time, been abandoned by lenders, as many believe. Also, FHA and VA fixed-rate loans should be available. In addition, as the interest and inflation rates peak, lenders will want to lock in borrowers at a fixed rate because these lenders will expect rates to decline in the future. At that point, the risk is shifted to the borrower and the lender will be in a situation 180 degrees opposite. Further, when the inflation rate and interest rates do subside to a stable level, institutions will again want to provide these fixed-rate loans since the proper atmosphere will exist for loans of this type. (See the earlier discussion.)

The "New" Mortgages

When interest rates are high, fixed-rate mortgages with their large monthly payments effectively price most potential homebuyers out of the market. In addition, lenders have been shying away from loaning funds for residential purchases due to their poor performance in attracting savings and their desire to shift the interest rate risk to the borrower. At the same time, prices are increasing rapidly, causing the total monthly payment to skyrocket.

Mortgage programs with such names as the Shared Appreciation Mortgage (SAM), the Piggyback Mortgage, the Pledged Account Mortgage (PAM), Variable Rate Mortgage (VRM), Renegotiable Rate Mortgage (RRM), Graduated Payment Mortgage (GPM), and others and combinations of these address the aforementioned concerns. Some primarily address the borrower's problem, others mainly the lender's problem; still others attempt to solve both parties' difficulties.

The SAM, GPM, PAM, and hybrids represent the best of the lot for the borrower and they will be discussed in detail. Some of the others are briefly discussed. Many of these plans are still in the finalization stage.

Shared Appreciation Mortgage (SAM)

This mortgage plan incorporates a loan amortized over 30 to 40 years with a fixed interest rate several points below the current market (often one-third less than the market). In return, the borrower agrees to share the potential appreciation with the lender when there is a sale, transfer, disposition, or refinancing of the property servicing the loan. (*Note:* Some SAM's require a sale or refinancing after 10 years.) Assuming the interest rate was one-third less than market, then the lender would share in one-third of the potential appreciation. Some of the loans are assumable and have been written without prepayment penalty clauses. (Of course, the homeowner has to address any appreciation at the time of sale and prior to the assumption.) In addition, if there is a 10 year maturity, guaranteed financing by the lender of the full outstanding principal plus the full amount of the contingent interest (the lender's share of the appreciation) would be stipulated if the property were not sold or refinanced prior to maturity (10 years).

SAM's are most helpful to those persons with income that otherwise would not qualify them to buy a home at current prices. Monthly payments are slashed to a manageable amount in many cases. To illustrate the effectiveness of a SAM, one study showed that only slightly more than 4% of U.S. households can qualify for a 16%, $60,000 mortgage. However, if a SAM was used, 13.6% of the households could then afford the same $60,000 mortgage.

Since this plan is new, there are still unresolved questions. Some of these include: Is the institution loaning the funds actually a lender or a partner? Assuming the institution is a lender, is the lender's share of the appreciation capital gain or ordinary income (interest) on the invested funds? If it is capital gain, the "lender" is treated very favorably tax-wise but the homebuyer has no interest deduction, which he would have had if the lender's share had been characterized as ordinary income. If the lender's share is treated as interest, very high effective lending rates are the result. Is this the equivalent of usury? If you refinance, how is the price term determined for the property?

All in all, the SAM has a bright future and as a buyer you should be aware of its existence, understand its operation, and investigate its applicability to your financial circumstances.

Graduated Payment Mortgage (GPM)

Actually, I am going to discuss one specific type of graduated mortgage. In fact, it is the only one that has really worked in the marketplace and it works *very well*.

First, however, let me describe the concept involved. Those that would have a difficult time qualifying today—especially the first time buyer or those seeking larger homes to accommodate a growing family but lack significant income—will find this program very attractive, assuming there is a reasonable expectation that income will increase with age and work experience. A GPM permits the borrower to pay lower than normal initial monthly payments during the early years of the loan when the borrower's income is low, with payments gradually increasing over the remaining life of the loan to a level above the conventional rate as the borrower's income increases. The monthly payment can increase by 2½, 5, or 7½% over five years (depending on the plan) or 2 or 3% per year over 10 years. The time period of the graduation of payments is fixed as is the interest rate over the life of the loan.

The most successful GPM has been the "piggyback" GPM. It gets its name from the fact that a second mortgage is "piggybacked" on the first mortgage. This is the critical distinction between it and the ordinary GPM. Here, all the variables of the GPM are built into the second mortgage. The first mortgage looks and acts like any other fixed-rate, 30 year amortized conventional mortgage. Thus, the secondary market, which buys mortgages/trust deeds in bulk from savings and loans and then resells them to private investors, welcomes this first mortgage. The second mortgage is written at a fixed rate several points above the first mortgage's rate. The second will compound negatively the first five years before stabilizing and amortizing over the 30 years. The borrower/homebuyer may prepay the second mortgage at any time without penalty or shorten the amortization and maturity on the second mortgage.

Using an example provided by the TIP Mortgage Corporation of Newport Beach, California, you can see how the piggyback GPM works. Assume you are buying a $116,300 house in California with 20% down. The loan amount is $93,000. Assuming conventional rates at 15½%, your monthly payment would be $1,214. With the TIP piggyback GPM, your initial payment would only be $1,001, rising 43.7% over the first five years to $1,438 and remaining at that point until maturity.

	Conventional Loan[a]	TIP Graduated Payment Mortgage[b]	
	---	---	---
Year	Monthly Payments	Monthly Payments	Principal Balance of First and Second Trust Deeds
1	$1,214	$1,001	$ 96,161
2	1,214	1,076	98,981
3	1,214	1,157	101,320
4	1,214	1,244	103,002
5	1,214	1,337	103,810
6	1,214	1,438	103,478
30	1,214	1,438	-0-

[a]Assume a $116,300 purchase price, 80% financed at 15.5%.
[b]Utilizing a combination first and second trust deed.

The only potential problem with the GPM is that in the first few years you are acquiring "negative amortization." That is, the amount that the lender deferred to keep early monthly payments low has been added to the principal amount outstanding. So you could owe more than you originally borrowed if you sell in this period. *However*, by choosing property wisely and by being in the market over this entire time period, your appreciation in the property will more than likely far outweigh the amount added to your original loan principal. The appropriateness of your decision to invest in the property should be proven out by your return on investment along with your tax savings accumulated over the years.

Shared Appreciation, Graduated Payment Mortgage

This plan, as it sounds, is a combination of two good plans. You, the borrower, and the lender agree to share the appreciation on the property after a number of years in return for an agreed upon below market interest rate for the buyer. After 7 or 10 years (whichever is agreed upon), the lender would get his share of the appreciation from the date of the purchase of the property. If you don't want to sell the property at this time, then you must refinance at current market rates for the remainder of the 30 year term. The lender's share of the appreciation at that point could be added to the remaining principal balance. In this manner, you don't have to come forward with any cash at that time. By adding this appreciation amount to the principal and by now paying full market interest rates, your monthly payments will be significantly higher. However, while your payment has graduated upward, hopefully your income has also.

Pledged Account Mortgage (PAM)

This mortgage is similar to a GPM in the sense that it permits lower initial monthly payments in the early years of home ownership. A PAM is sometimes known as a "buy-down"—that is, you are "buying down" the interest rate to a more manageable level. There are two forms of this PAM—the buyer buy-down and the ordinary developer/builder buy-down.

The Buyer Buy-Down. In the first case, you take part of your down payment (10% or more) and deposit it into a savings account with the mortgage lender and pledge it as additional collateral against the loan. In return for a reduction in the interest rate of three percentage points (or more), the lender will monthly draw down the account (in increments of $150 or more in the first year). After the first and second years, smaller amounts may be deducted from the account if out-of-pocket payments increase. By the end of the third year, the account has a zero balance and is now paying full market interest. The attraction of this mortgage is the lower payments in the initial years, rising to market over three years, matching household income growth patterns. Second, you are able to qualify for the loan based on the discounted interest rate monthly payment and not based on the total payments at current rates. Thus, more people can qualify for this type of loan than some others.

Developer/Builder Buy-Down. The other type of buy-down is becoming very common today. Builders are stuck with more and more homes and they need to sell them quickly or go broke. One technique to do this is for the builder/developer to offer lower financing for the first three years. He uses the same PAM plan as outlined previously, except he goes to the lender and arranges for the buy-down. The builder in this case supplies the difference between the discounted rate mortgage payment and what would have been the actual monthly payment. Builder/developers who participate in this type of mortgage are allowed to pay the lender any amount up to $150 per month in the first year. In the second and third years, these payments would decrease in equal amounts.

The buyer and builder programs could be combined, making monthly payments significantly lower. But, even so, the builder's subsidization is not to be taken into account in qualifying you for the loan.

Flexible Payment Mortgage (FPM)

The FPM is a plan whereby you, the borrower, pay interest only on the loan in the first five years. The original principal amount remains constant during this five year period. The underlying loan is the fixed-rate, long-term type.

At the end of the five year period, payments are increased by a sufficient amount to allow for both principal and interest payments that will fully amortize (pay off) the entire balance at the end of the term of the mortgage.

Again, the plan is good for those with moderate current incomes but with expectations of certain earnings increases in future years. It will get you into the house. However, the negative feature is that at the end of the five year initial period, your monthly payments will be significantly higher and you will have to be able to meet those payments.

Renegotiable Rate Mortgage (RRM) or Rollover Mortgage (ROM)

In this plan, the lender will fix an interest rate for a period (usually for only three to five years at a time), even though the lender makes a long-term commitment. At the end of each period, the mortgage is renegotiated at a rate that reflects the current market rates more adequately. The lender is under an obligation to renew the mortgage at the appropriate adjustment time, without prepayment penalties or extra fees.

The interest rate can be increased or decreased no more than 5% over the life of the mortgage. The rate can increase or decrease a maximum in one period of ½% per year multiplied by the number of years in the period, up to the maximum permitted. For example, if the term was five years, the maximum increase at the end of that term would be 2½%. Thus, a 12½% loan would then be at 15% for the next five years.

At the time of this writing, the lender is required to give you three months notice prior to your agreed term date of the new interest rate. That rate is pegged to the Monthly National Average Mortgage Rate Index for all mortgage lenders. This is a very short-term index and, thus, is more sensitive to interest rate changes. This, in turn, means that if rates are increasing generally, a loan pegged to this rate will reflect a greater percentage of that increase than an interest rate pegged to an index of a longer term—say six months or a year. This volatility in interest rate changes is one of the problems with this and other Variable Rate Mortgages (VRM's), and this point will be discussed further in the VRM section below.

It can be said, however, that because of the relative length of the period (3 to 5 years) prior to a rate change, and the fact that the amount of change is restricted to certain levels, this represents the best of the genre known as VRM's. It should also be noted that it is *possible* for rates to decline, although not very probable over certain periods. Also, as with all of these instruments, it may be that the holding period of your investment is only two or three years. Thus, these changes in rates may diminish in importance to you. The main idea is to get into the property. If the plan helps you do that it is a good one.

Variable Rate Mortgage (VRM)

VRM's are of two types, restricted and unrestricted. Let's talk about the restricted or "California" plan, since this is where this kind of plan originated. (However, note that the State of California now permits state-chartered financial institutions to make unrestricted VRM's, similar to federally chartered institutions.)

The Restricted VRM. The California VRM represents an attempt to make consumers and lenders happy. The mortgage is long-term, with fixed monthly payments over specified five year periods. However, the interest rate charged during these periods can vary. Every six months the rate can be adjusted upward by .25%, with a maximum of 2½% over the life of the mortgage. The rate can be adjusted downward by any amount. The interest rate change is based on an interest rate index change. If the index increases near the .25% range or more for the six month period, the interest rate charged will be adjusted upward. The restricted plan thus allows for a sharing of the inflation related risks between lender and borrower—each gets some protection.

The Unrestricted VRM. The unrestricted VRM represents the worst of all evils for the consumer. True, it probably will make some money available for mortgages, but the point will be moot since no one could afford to make the payments over time. The unrestricted VRM is similar to the aforementioned VRM except that interest rates can be adjusted to any level at any time (even monthly) as long as those changes are based on a published interest rate index that is not under the lender's control. Some of these indexes include four recommended by the Federal Home Loan Bank Board: Lenders' Cost of Funds Index, the Average Contract Mortgage Rate Index, the yield on three and six month Treasury bills, and rates paid by the Treasury to buyers of Treasury notes and bonds. The choice of index is critical, since the longer the term of the index, the more stable it is. The more stable the index, the less likely are wide fluctuations in interest rate adjustments on your mortgage.

To show the effect on monthly payments, a purchaser of a $75,000 home (placing 20% down) in 1978 could have had 3 (Cost of Funds Index) to 8.5 (3 Month Treasury Bill Index) percentage points added to the interest rate. That is, a 9.25% interest loan could have risen to 12.25% all the way to 17.75%. The purchaser's monthly payment would have jumped from about $494 to anywhere from $629 to $895. Obviously, if you obtain this type of loan, seek one tied to a long-term index and try to find a VRM with a cap on interest rate increases.

Some of the savings and loans have announced that they will limit interest rate increases to 7.5% or some other figure per year. This is not much consolation to you because 7.5% is a *large* increase. Further, VRM's, because of the nature of fixed payments for periods of time with simultaneous interest rate increases, result in negative amortization. Since the payments more than likely won't cover all that owed due to the elevated interest, the difference is added to the principal balance. This means you could owe a much larger amount of principal (especially with the unrestricted plan.) Note, though, that at the end of the five year periods, the monthly payment amounts would be raised to try to avoid this situation. That being the case, unless competition steps in to limit the interest rate hikes and their frequency, I venture to say that this plan will not be popular and some other mortgage solution will have to be found.

The unrestricted VRM is an attempt to shift all of the interest rate risk to the borrower. It is the opposite situation of the fixed-rate loan where the *lender* bears all of the risk.

There are a few advantages to the VRM. First, it is assumable. Second, the borrower can prepay at each five year readjustment (to reduce payments) without penalty. Third, the VRM is usually offered with an initial rate under that of a fixed-rate loan—some 3 to 5 points. Finally, a buyer can qualify for a 95% loan as opposed to an 80 to 90% loan with a fixed-rate mortgage.

To recap, I have outlined several of the new mortgage plans. After reading about them, you should notice that they are discussed in order of their help to you. That is, the SAM and GPM are the most helpful and the unrestricted VRM the least. You should investigate all, however. If it means getting into the house, take the loan. You can later refinance, sell, or possibly, exchange up. Get into the market!

Creative Financing

Even if you can't qualify for a mortgage loan for some reason you are not stuck yet. There are other considerations.

Use of a Cosigner

Consider having another responsible person cosign the loan. The lender thus has more security should you fail to pay some or all of the indebtedness, in that there is another person to look to for payment. The cosigner is in effect a type of guarantor of the loan payment.

Assumable Mortgages

You would probably do better to seek out properties with assumable mortgages (the detailed proforma at the end of Part II contemplates this situation). There are, and will continue to be, a number of them out there, at very attractive interest rates. This is true despite the recent U.S. Supreme Court ruling regarding the enforceability of the due-on-sale clause. In fact, in addition to the supply of mortgages which presently do not include due-on-sale clauses, lenders may determine that it is desirable to permit you to assume a mortgage, provided that you bear some of the risk. For example, the mortgage instrument might provide for an increase in the interest rate of a few points or provide for a renegotiaged rate. However, the new rate may still be several points under the current market rate of interest.

An assumable loan might carry an interest rate of 9¾% (10% APR), whereas a new conventional loan and mortgage/trust deed would cost you, as of this writing, between 14 to 16%. This translates into a difference in monthly principal and interest payments of between $157 and $234 on a $48,000 loan. At 9¾% (10% APR) interest for 30 years, the monthly principal and interest is $421 as opposed to $578 at 14% (14¼% APR) interest, and $655 at 16% (16¼% APR). It stands to reason that you should qualify much easier at a lower interest rate than at a higher one, since the gross income necessary to support the lower payment would be significantly less.

Even if the supply of assumable mortgages dried up completely, the program outlined in this guide remains intact. Of course, if interest rates are higher, then it is somewhat more difficult to qualify as previously mentioned. At the same time, however, the amount of tax write-off increases.

Wraparound Mortgage

Consider attempting to find a seller who will sell subject to an all-inclusive trust deed (or wraparound mortgage). An illustration is the best way to explain this useful device. The seller conveys his property to you for $110,000 subject to a first mortgage lien of $75,000 at 9% annual interest. You give the seller $10,000 in cash (down payment) and a promissory note for $100,000, which is secured by a second mortgage on the property. This note bears interest at 13% annually. Since the $100,000 promissory note "includes" the unpaid liability of $75,000 (secured by the first mortgage), the purchase money note and mortgage are said to be "wrapped around" the first mortgage. You make payments to the seller on the $100,000, and the seller continues to pay the bank the required amount on the $75,000 first mortgage.

These wraparound mortgages are very popular in tight money and high interest rate markets. They provide advantages to both the buyer and seller.

Advantages to the buyer.
1. It could be easier to qualify for this transaction, because it is then a case of convincing an individual seller instead of a financial institution that you can carry the financial burden. An individual generally is not going to require the detail that a bank or other institution insists upon.
2. The down payment may be less than that required otherwise.
3. The interest rate may be less than in a conventional loan origination or even an assumable loan.

Advantages to the seller.
1. The seller gets the property sold, which may be difficult in a tight money or high interest rate market.
2. The seller has additional security in that the bank will not foreclose without notice to him since he is still paying the interest on the first mortgage.

3. Use of the device may avoid activation of a due-on-sale clause (discussed earlier) on the first mortgage, thus allowing the lower-interest first mortgage to be preserved. (This is obviously an advantage to you also.) The bank/savings and loan may not know that a transfer of possession and title have been made, since the seller is continuing to send to the bank payments on the first mortgage, utilizing the seller's own checks. However, you should be aware that this potential advantage could be lost, since more and more financial institutions are looking beyond the name of the payment check. (For example, they might inspect title to the property.) If the institution does discover the transfer and you do not meet the state tests (regarding impairment of security and risk of default) or if the first mortgage is held by a federally chartered savings and loan unwilling to permit the first mortgage to be preserved (even at a renegotiated rate), this financing device will be unavailable.

4. The rate of return is significant for the seller. In the aforementioned example, the seller is receiving 13% on the $25,000 (the $110,000 purchase price less the down payment less the $75,000 first mortgage) and a "spread" of 4% (13–9%) on the $75,000 first mortgage (or the equivalent of 12% on $25,000) for a total rate of return of 25% on the $25,000 amount, which he still has in the property.

Second Trust Deeds

If the seller's loan is assumable or you can only qualify for a certain loan amount, and there remains a gap between the price of the house and the sum of the down payment and first mortgage/trust deed, the seller can take back a fixed-rate second mortgage/trust deed for the difference. Generally, this will be at a lower than market rate since the seller's motivation is not to be a lender but to sell his house. Your total mortgage payments will be less than on a new first mortgage on the total funds borrowed.

There are pitfalls to be aware of. First, many second trust deeds have very short terms, although they may be amortized over 30 years. Thus, in three to five years you would have a large "balloon" payment to make. If the home doesn't appreciate much for some reason and lenders continue to avoid the mortgage market, you won't be able to refinance your loan. Second, the true price of the house is usually distorted when the seller takes back paper. That is, if you pay $110,000 for a house and receive a $10,000 second mortgage, the real price is $100,000. (The seller has adjusted his price for the second.) However, the broker gets a commission on the full $110,000. (The seller pays the commission.) Third, if the tax assessor uses the selling price to determine property taxes, you are going to be hit with higher tax bills, in this case by 10%.

Contract of Sale

You might use a contract of sale to your benefit. A contract of sale (or "contract for deed") is an agreement to convey title to property only upon fulfillment of specified conditions. Until that time, the seller retains title to the property.

Assuming your income is not high enough to qualify for a loan at this time for one reason or another, but will be in the future, you should consider this device. This device allows you to freeze the price of the home, but simultaneously delay the closing for a long time—until your income level is sufficient to qualify for the requisite loan amount and/or interest rates have dropped.

Aside from the down payment, you can move into the property with only monthly rental payments, a part of which may be applied to the price of the property when escrow does close. The seller, as in the case of the wraparound mortgage, will continue to be liable for payments due on the existing mortgages. You become an "equitable" owner with possessory rights to the property.

The aforementioned assumable loans, wraparounds, second mortgages/trust deeds, and land sale contracts are some of the "creative financing" techniques presently used. Actually, "creative financing" is a misnomer. These techniques are not very creative or very new, but are more popular when there is a tight money squeeze. In a recent tight money period some estimates place 80% of residential sales in metropolitan markets using one or more of these devices.

5

Other Opportunities

Okay, you don't have a rich uncle, no one wants to lend you *that* much money, and/or you don't have quite enough for that large down payment. Nothing has worked. Give up? I hope not. For those of you who know that ownership of real estate is the key, but lack the financial means, there are several more avenues to explore. Some of these may not appeal to you, but don't let your ego ruin your long-term financial future. Remember, look at the real estate as an investment and tax-saving device. It's better to own a *small*, solid investment than none at all. The following can represent your start up the real estate pyramid.

Manufactured Housing and Mobile Homes

Manufactured housing and mobile homes conjure up very bad images in the minds of some people. However, these types of shelter have made vast strides in terms of their appeal and quality of construction and their growing attractiveness to lenders. Further, manufactured housing is, in some localities, accorded nearly the same rights as standard residential construction. The result is that the manufactured house in these areas will be permitted wherever conventional single-family homes can be located. Prices of manufactured housing range from $20,000 to $70,000 (in California) not including the price of the lot. The lot should cost approximately $20,000 to $25,000 (in California), and the foundation, yard, driveway, garage, etc., should cost about $10,000. Therefore, an 1,800 square foot manufactured home could be purchased for $70,000 as opposed to a minimum of $135,000 for the average new conventional home in an outlying area. The primary reason that the manufactured house is only one-half the cost of the conventional home is the economies effected in modular assembly-line factory construction.

Also, multi-family, multi-story manufactured housing is available. Thus, condominium units, which generally are less expensive than a similarly sized house, can be purchased. For example, a project in Palmdale, California, features 252 townhomes in 83 buildings. The units came on the market in April 1981 with two and three bedroom models, ranging from 1,080 to 1,200 square feet. Prices ranged from $49,900 to $57,900.

Mobile home subdivision parks are being developed in significant numbers at this time. Including a 6,000 to 8,000 square foot lot, with a home of 1,400 to 1,500 square feet, you could pay a total price of as low as $50,000. These homes appreciate in value in the same manner as conventional housing, in areas where these developments are popular, such as the Phoenix, Arizona, metropolitan area. These developments offer other attractions, however. Normally, these parks include a clubhouse with meeting and game rooms, a kitchen, and billiard/pool tables. Also a pool and jacuzzi are offered to residents. Other amenities could include shuffleboard and tennis courts, planned social activities, golf courses/putting greens, etc.

Housing for the Elderly

In many cases a senior citizen can do better, that is, get more living space and amenities for his dollar, by buying a home located in a retirement community. These developments are planned specifically for the senior citizen's lifestyle. Because many of them are built on massive amounts of acreage, they are generally located in outlying sections of metropolitan areas where land is inexpensive. This lower cost land, the economics of scale producing similar but distinct homes, and cost savings that result from design of a house suited for seniors, allows the developer to reduce the price of the home.

Leisure World and Sun City were pioneers of this concept and have been extremely successful. Others have copied that success. Typical of the new developments is the Highland Lakes development in Florida. It comprises 1,600 acres and is close to Tampa. In 1981, prices ranged from approximately $50,000 for a condominium to about $80,000 for a single-family residence.

These developments also satisfy other basic needs such as mixing with other persons of like age and desires. Activities are planned and recreational facilities are available to residents. It is not uncommon to see persons in the Sun City, Arizona, retirement community driving in golf carts along the street to the golf course, to friends' homes, to shopping, etc. Evenings at these developments are far from dull. In fact, with square dancing nights, big band nights, bingo, and so on, these communities are much more active than others in the metropolitan area.

Many of these developments are planned in the future in response to the rapidly increasing number of senior citizens. By 1990, this number should swell to over 40 million persons (a 19% increase). This represents a larger growth rate than that of the general population (15%). Hopefully, the laws of supply and demand will work in your favor. If developers rush into these developments (the profit is much better than in other housing developments), competitive forces will keep the prices at an affordable level for a while.

Home Conversions

To make purchase more attainable, many people have legally or illegally converted their single-family houses into two-unit houses. The U.S. Census figures have indicated more than 500,000 unexpected additional housing units. (All of these were the result of conversions without appropriate building permits.) Split-level houses are particularly suited for this type of conversion. The rent charged for the unit can assist you in your monthly payments.

I want to stress that I am not advising you to undertake illegal house conversions. If a legal conversion is permitted in your community, you may want to consider this alternative. I do believe that these conversions are becoming commonplace and vast in number and that some cities will move to legalize these conversions, as has Princeton, New Jersey. The officials in cities will move to legalize conversion so as to permit them to insure proper construction. Furthermore, a great deal of additional rental units could be forthcoming to help alleviate the rental housing shortage. For example, if only 1% of all homes in California in R-1 zones were converted, 50,000 more rental units would result.

The primary disadvantage of a conversion is that your privacy is affected to a degree, depending on the tenants. You will have to do a good job of screening tenants. (See Chapter 11.)

Rent (Lease) with Option to Buy

In this case, you can buy time now in order to afford a house in the future. That is, while working on raising a down payment, you can be living in a house. Part of the monthly lease payment reflects an amount in excess of the market rent. This amount is the option payment. You are paying for an option—an option that gives you the right to purchase specific property (the house) for a certain price. However, you have control over the seller's property and the resulting appreciation for generally very low amounts of cash. (You have locked in the price of the home.)

Why does a seller grant lease options? First, there are tax benefits, whereby the cash he receives for the option usually will not be taxed for some time in the future thus also aiding his general cash flow. Second, the additional cash (for the option) may cover any negative pre-tax cash flow he would have had if he had merely rented the unit to a tenant. Third, in a difficult economic market, the seller has been able to "sell" the house.

Negotiable Broker's Fees

It is a popular misconception that real estate brokers are to be compensated a standard 6% commission. Broker's fees *are* negotiable and, in recent legal cases, courts have upheld this concept. Therefore, if the seller has negotiated a better rate with his broker, attempt to persuade the seller to lower his price and/or the down payment by this amount. One or two percent of a $100,000 house is $1,000 to $2,000. If he lowers the price of the house by $2,000, your down payment drops by $400 (assuming a 20% down payment) and your loan amount drops by $1,600. Thus, up-front money as well as monthly payments could be less. Or, the seller could keep the price of the house at $100,000 but lower the down payment from $20,000 to $18,000 (assuming the lender agrees) to reflect the amount already in his pocket.

6

Title

There are several additional ways to hold property with others, aside from those previously discussed. Each has its own set of rules, advantages, and disadvantages.

Tenants in Common

If you hold title as "tenants in common," each of you can report a proportionate share of gross income, deductible expenses, and gains/losses on disposition of the property. Note that if one or the other tenant in common pays a larger part of the expenses, the above rule still applies. Also note that "proportionate share" is measured by the capital contribution of each. For example, if three people each contribute $4,000 to the total $12,000 initial cost, then each is liable for one-third of the costs, and each would report one-third of the gross income and deductible expenses, and each would have a one-third share of the gain/loss on disposition of the property.

Joint Tenants

If title is held as "joint tenants," each joint tenant can report only so much of the deductible expenses as he actually pays, even though each joint tenant reports his proportionate share of gross income and gains/losses on disposition. There is a good reason for the difference in treatment. As opposed to the situation where each tenant in common is only personally liable for his proportionate share of the expenses, a joint tenant is personally liable for the total expenses incurred. There is another difference when title is taken as joint tenants. In a joint tenancy with right of survivorship, upon the death of the first joint tenant, the property interest held by the decedent automatically goes to the surviving joint tenant without going through the probate procedure. The decedent has given up his right to testamentary disposition (disposition by will) of the property and, in effect, the survivor has full legal title to the property.

Title Between Spouses

Before I continue discussing other forms of taking title, let me discuss the situation when husband and wife buy real property. A couple may own real property in several different ways: as tenants in common, joint tenants, tenancy by the entirety (where permitted), as community property (where permitted), or in the name of the spouse who paid for it. Since the manner of ownership does not affect the right to split income on the joint income tax return, it really does not matter which way they hold the property as far as federal income taxes go—with one exception.

On the death of one of the spouses, if the property is held in joint tenancy, only one-half of the property (the decedent's interest) is given a stepped-up basis (to fair market value), whereas if the property were held as community property, both halves receive the step-up in basis. This is critical when the asset is later sold, in that basis is a vital element in determining gain/loss on disposition of property.

And, with the passage of the Economic Recovery Tax Act of 1981, federal gift taxes between spouses is a moot point. Thus, a spouse could purchase a property with his own separate funds and take title as tenants in common, as community property, or as joint tenants without incurring federal gift tax liability even though he has, in effect, made a gift of one-half of the real property to his spouse. He winds up federal gift tax-wise in the same position had he taken title in his name alone. (Note, however, state gift tax law may still regard the aforementioned transfer as a taxable gift of one-half and this should be considered.)

However, the form of title held between spouses may make a big difference with regard to estate tax matters. For example, if the property is held in the purchasing spouse's sole name (and the purchasing spouse paid for the property solely out of his own funds), the deceased spouse's estate would include the entire property. However, if title is taken as tenants in common, as community property, or as joint tenants, then only one-half of the property is included in the decedent's estate and, thus, estate taxes are lowered. (Of course, in light of the new Act, spouses can significantly reduce or even eliminate estate taxes through the use of proper estate planning.)

Probate Procedures

As mentioned earlier, property held in joint tenancy does not go through the probate procedure. "Probate" is a court proceeding designed to clear title to property passing under the will or by intestacy (where there is no will). It is a matter of public record and normally involves various costs and delays. The "right of survivorship" feature of joint tenancy permits the property, upon the death of the first joint tenant, to be passed directly to the surviving joint tenant. The same property owned by persons as tenants in common would not enjoy the same treatment, but instead would be subject to probate. Whereas previously community property had to be probated, in many cases this is no longer necessary. In California, where the property interest is held as community property, and passes directly to the surviving spouse, a brief "set-aside" proceeding is available through the Probate Court. This procedure basically confirms the community property to the survivor without the full probate proceeding. It is quick and relatively efficient. Thus, avoiding probate is possible through either use of joint tenancy title *or* community property.

The married reader in particular can see, without a continued discussion of the subject, that he must consider more than just income taxes when purchasing a property. I will leave the remaining discussion of estate and gift tax liability in regard to form of ownership of property by marrieds and others, and the relative advantages and disadvantages, to your own competent real estate and tax attorneys. However, in reference to joint tenancy title, some of its drawbacks are outlined in Chapter 30.

Corporate Ownership

In addition to the aforementioned ways to hold title, you could establish a corporation and the corporation could purchase the property. However, the seeming advantages of lower tax rates (16% on the first $25,000 of taxable income, dropping to 15% in 1983 and beyond; 19% on the next $25,000, 18% in 1983 and beyond; 20% on the next $25,000; 40% on the next $25,000; and 46% on the remainder) and possible limited liability are offset by:

1. The double taxation (on income earned and then on dividends paid);
2. The fact that the deductions are the corporation's and are not passed through to the shareholders (similarly for losses);
3. The income not paid to the shareholder can be used only for corporate purposes (and not the individual's);
4. The fact that, in a small corporation, a shareholder's personal assets most likely will not be sheltered from payment for unsatisfied corporate debts and legal suits.

Either financial institutions and vendors will require that the shareholders sign documents individually or, at a later date upon an unsatisfied claim, a suit could be commenced whereby a cause of action will seek to "pierce the corporate veil" by alleging that the corporation is merely an "alter ego" of the shareholder.

Thus, this device will not help you reach your objective of lowering your present taxable income and, in turn, income taxes on that income. Even sub-chapter S corporations which basically allow profit/loss pass through to the shareholders have strict operating restrictions as to amounts of passive income, rents, dividends, and special rules regarding holding periods for capital gains treatment and a penalty for failure to comply (possible taxation of the gain at the *corporate* rate). Furthermore, you might also end up paying more tax because of various restrictions in the Code, such as those that relate to personal holding companies.

A corporate form of ownership requires particular attention to detail. There is another entity, the Real Estate Investment Trust, which resembles a corporation that owns real property. However, the Real Estate Investment Trust is not subject to corporate income taxes provided that it distributes at least 95% of its cash flow to investors. Because of the close scrutiny by the SEC and the states, and the disclosure requirements (and attendant time and cost), this is not really a viable alternative in light of the scale on which you will operate.

I would make one suggestion on all of the aforementioned material: if you are engaging in the program outlined in this guide, it would seem that the corporate form of ownership is not very attractive and generally should be avoided for purposes of owning real estate.

It should be evident to you by now that a motivated person will find down payment funds and loans for which he can qualify. He will find the correct kind of property to fit his circumstances. And he will hold title to that property in the most beneficial manner.

In Part II, I will discuss what is involved in using the technique I propose.

Part II

The Technique

7

Introduction to the Technique

The technique involves the systematic purchase of single family houses to be used as rental income properties (and the proper disposition of such—discussed in Part IV), as well as the optimum utilization of deductions. Sounds simple, right? Actually it is, as long as you pay attention to detail. You must approach this activity as a business. The houses must be purchased at the right price, in the proper location, at the right time. They must be operated as legitimate rental units with proper management. They must later be disposed of at the right time, in the proper manner, and to the proper party. Deductions must be maximized in view of existing tax laws.

Remember, your primary purpose is the operation of rental housing in such a way as to reduce income taxes and maximize your after-tax dollars. Thus, you can be increasing your gross income, your spendable income, and your net wealth, as well as decreasing the overall negative impact of inflation.

There are many considerations involved in this technique. Some of the more important of these include the following:

1. Location and type of property.
2. Type of purchase approach.
3. Management of the property.

4. Tenants.
5. Operating expenses and other considerations.
6. Interest and casualty loss expenses.
7. Depreciation.

The following chapters will deal with the aforementioned eight items, making reference to the proforma found at the end of this Part. This proforma details the results from a hypothetical investment in a $60,000 house in northwest Houston. The holding period utilized in the proforma was two years, but this decision must be made in light of various factors, including your own financial circumstances. Note that the hypothetical investor in the proforma is in the 50% tax bracket.

If you do not presently own any real property, your first move might be to get yourself out of a rental unit, if possible, and into ownership of your personal residence. If you do, you will accomplish several financial objectives, aside from the personal freedom and satisfaction derived from home ownership itself. First, the deductions associated with the home will generally allow you to exceed the "zero bracket amount" in the Code (as previously discussed) and, thus, ensure the maximum offset against your ordinary income. You will have started on the road to lowering your tax bill. Second, your monthly payments will be going toward something concrete, of which you will receive a share—the equity—which amounts to the initial down payment and the appreciation in the value of the home.

Assume you live in a state such as California, where much of the housing is beyond the reach of the average taxpayer. My suggestion, if you could raise maybe $12,000 but not the $20,000 to $30,000 necessary for a down payment on a home in California, is to purchase a good $50,000 to $60,000 home in a sunbelt state. I specifically mention the sunbelt states (as opposed to other areas of the country) because of their long-term growth potential which should be reflected in higher appreciation of the house. These houses do exist—in my travels I have seen them. Rent the house out. You should accomplish even more than if you bought the house for your own personal use since you can take depreciation and operating expense deductions in addition to interest, taxes, and the other normal itemized deductions. As your property appreciates and your income rises, then make your next step by purchasing a personal residence or another income-producing property. (Part III will detail the effect on taxes in a typical purchase program).

8

Location and Type of Property

Location Criteria

As previously mentioned, you should concentrate primarily on the sunbelt states: California, Texas, Arizona, and New Mexico, in particular. In addition, other isolated states may have potential for one reason or another. For example, some states are experiencing booms due to exploration and development of energy. In this instance, Colorado may be a good place. Similarly, certain areas are benefitting from other phenomena; for example, Florida, with the influx of immigrants, many of whom are wealthy, has turned from a state with an oversupply of housing to one where housing is in demand.

The point is that you must do your homework in selecting areas for your purchases. Following are some key aspects to be aware of.

Rent Control

Purchase real property in major metropolitan areas that do not have rent control laws. Most rent controls exempt single-family houses, but it is better to avoid the problem, if possible. Contrary to what most people think, rent control affects *all* the property in the area. It directly affects those buildings falling within the rent control ordinance by lowering the property values of such buildings. Since future rent increases are limited, these properties become less desirable to investors. In many cases, the owners of such buildings will allow them to deteriorate because they cannot cover costs. This makes the area look bad and all property values tend to suffer.

Since the property values of the rent controlled buildings are diminished significantly, smart owners seek property tax relief and often obtain it. Unfortunately, this shifts a greater tax burden onto other property owners.

Time and time again, experience has shown that these areas attract a greater number of low-income (or no income) persons and an increase in crime. In extreme cases, rental buildings are abandoned or converted to other uses—parking/vacant lots or, sometimes, condominiums—if the area still has some viability.

Employment Potential

Look for areas where major employers are building plants, warehouses, and offices since people necessary to fill the jobs created will require housing and, the longer the trend continues, the larger the appreciation of the property (as long as the area is not overbuilt). Also, look for areas with a *diverse* industrial and business base. This type of market can withstand a decline in any one industry by offsetting it with gains in others.

Contrast this with a city like Detroit, Michigan. It is a great city. However, it is heavily (and overly) dependent on the automotive industry. When the auto companies are in a slump, Detroit suffers. Presently, as I write this guide, people are leaving Detroit and places like it in great numbers because no jobs are available. Don't invest in one-horse (one industry) towns, even if things are booming at the time you investigate those areas. Eventually this selection will kill you. As a small investor, you cannot afford this type of risk taking.

Vacancy Rates

Avoid areas with a significant amount of unsold houses and areas with a high rental vacancy rate. Either will cause your own vacancy factor to reflect a higher rate. Remember, you are trying to avoid vacancy. High vacancy causes *real* losses. Real losses (as opposed to paper losses) are the worst thing that can happen to you.

Climate

Seek areas with favorable climates, both meteorological and business. Both will help to attract people and new employers. Note, though, that the mere fact that an area has warm weather much of the year does not automatically make it a prime candidate for investment. That is, I seem to remember from my engineering school days that it takes more energy to cool a house than to heat it. Since energy is in short supply and increasingly more expensive, it is imperative to find geographic locations that are the least burdensome to the investor's pocketbook. Otherwise, future growth in that market will be jeopardized.

As to the optimum business climate, an area that has a low or no corporate tax (or for that matter low taxes in general) will be most desirable to business, all other things being equal. If the local and state governments do not over-regulate this will help to attract new industry. Without businesses and industry, there is no employment base. Without that base, there will be few persons living in the area.

Also, watch out for no-growth policy areas. For example, the city of Camarillo in Ventura County, California, recently enacted an ordinance limiting the number of housing units that can be built within its borders. This type of policy will absolutely drive business to other communities.

Energy Exploration

Seek areas that have a solid energy exploration base, as previously mentioned. Of course, you must weigh this factor with the others, but the oil drilling activity in Texas and oil shale exploration in Colorado make places like Houston, Dallas, and Denver seem very attractive because they already rank well in other site location criteria. However, smaller places like Wheatland and Wright, Wyoming, or Zap, North Dakota, would not be good investment areas, despite their strong energy bases (coal, oil, etc.). They fail for other reasons. They are one-horse towns. This type of place booms for a while, then inevitably becomes an economic bust.

Defense Contracts

Watch for areas that are home to the major defense contractors. Those areas with presently solid business bases should be more attractive in the future as strengthening our military capability commands more attention and many billions of dollars. However, be careful to analyze where bid-winning contractors plan to perform the work on their contracts. That is the key.

For example, a defense contractor headquartered in Los Angeles may subcontract most of the work to companies in foreign countries. This does not make Los Angeles look all that more attractive than before. It helps some, but not as much as if the actual engineering and construction of the armaments had taken place in Los Angeles.

Other Indicators

Look for other indicators that will draw people and/or employers to an area. This does not mean that you must concentrate in only one of these states or only in the sunbelt states. Other isolated areas may suit you for one reason or another. You might want to diversify and buy in several states, thus spreading your risk. (The risk is that one real estate market may experience slow or no growth or even negative growth at certain times).

In the proforma and for purposes of this discussion, I have selected a target area of northwestern Houston, Texas. This area has demonstrated significant growth in terms of people and jobs over the past several years, and this growth seems to be continuing. The appreciation in residential real property in these years has approximated 15% annually. The business climate is very favorable: (a) there are no state corporate income taxes, (b) the state welcomes business and provides assistance to companies in search of a location, etc., (c) it is a diversified economy, and (d) there is a strong energy base. People are flocking to Texas to escape cold winters experienced in other areas. Furthermore, there are no state/ local income taxes and Houston is near the bottom of a list of the 40 largest cities, as far as the cost of living is concerned.

Research the Market Area

After determining your own criteria for selecting the most desirable areas, you should then use as many sources of information as possible to measure each market's actual performance against these criteria.

Newspapers

You should start with the local newspapers. They have real estate sections that will give you some hint as to real estate activity in the area. The business section will be a reflection of the local economy. Similarly, any specialized business newspapers (e.g., *Houston Business Journal*) will be of great assistance in measuring business activity. The general news sections will reflect the quality of life in the market.

Planning Agencies

The local Chamber of Commerce and regional and local planning agencies can supply you with demographic data. For example, data on population (amount, location, distribution by age, sex, race, etc.), income (where better income areas are located, median income), and employment by type and source are generally available. Also, don't overlook the U.S. Censuses of Population and Business which are available in many libraries. The latter provides a plethora of business indicators such as retail sales by area.

Realtors

Check with realtors active in the market. Since they operate there on a day-to-day basis, who would be a better judge of the area? Of course, you must inquire very discretely. Otherwise, you will get biased answers. After all, who isn't prejudiced when it comes to their own home town?

Owners' Associations

Income property owner organizations should be contacted. For example, there is normally an apartment owners' association in major areas. Since they deal with landlord/tenant relations regularly, a wealth of information on vacancy rates and patterns, types of tenants, types of buildings/properties, locations of better rental areas, etc., can be obtained. In fact, just by talking with this group you will learn an important fact. That is, you should be able to discern the relative strength and impact of the organization in the area. The stronger the organization, the more desirable the market.

Use any data you can get your hands on. But don't expect to complete the process in a short time. The more thorough your analysis, the more likely you are to select the proper area that meets or exceeds your investment location criteria.

Visits

Finally, to check your work and satisfy your curiosity, you should plan a trip to the few markets you believe are best for you. Only then are you ready to make your decision with a reasonable measure of confidence.

Type of Property

The technique proposes the purchase of single family houses as opposed to multi-unit buildings for several reasons. First, the cost is generally less for a house than a multi-unit building and, thus, you can more readily afford the house. Second, unless you have experience in the real property rental area, you will not want to take too large a bite the first time out. Instead, get your feet wet in the program. It may be, for a variety of reasons, that you won't or can't continue in this type of program in the future. Third, any problems experienced would only be magnified in a multi-unit situation. You note that there will most likely be *some* problems, as in any situation. However, with the proper professional assistance, they should be minimized.

New Houses

You should purchase houses that are new or nearly new; this eliminates most major maintenance expense problems. However, this does *not* mean that the house should not be inspected thoroughly before you and the seller enter into a purchase and sale. If you personally don't make, or can't make, a detailed inspection from the basement (or ground) up, then hire any one of many reputable inspection firms. For a relatively nominal sum, they will check everything and provide you with a written summary of the condition of the house. This could save you a great deal of money and headaches in the long run, either by eliminating from your consideration a house with major defects (possibly hidden) or by providing solid positive information on a house about which you originally had your doubts.

Amenities

The houses should and usually do have amenities such as central air conditioning, all built-in appliances, fireplaces, large yards (hopefully fenced) and three or four bedrooms. They should be located in appealing subdivisions with, if possible, common areas with pools, tennis courts, etc. (operated by a community association). The subdivisions should be located in growth areas with good access to major freeways and local roads. The subdivisions should also be located near schools and major employment and retail centers. The aforementioned will make the property more attractive to prospective renters and cause the value of the property to rise over time.

Assumable Loans

As I discussed in Part I, you should seek houses with assumable loans carrying interest rates between 8 and 10% (or slightly higher), and be willing and able to pay a minimum of 20% of the purchase price as a down payment ($12,000 on a $60,000 house). (There will be some other associated sales costs and you should have, as a reserve, up to 3 or 4% of the purchase price to cover such expenses.)

9

Type of Purchase Approach

In the detailed proforma, and for purposes of this discussion, you will be purchasing $60,000 houses using what I characterize as the *aggressive* posture. That is, you have decided that your strategy is to buy the property with as little down payment as possible. Your monthly payments will most likely be greater than the rent received, thus producing a negative cash flow. In the detailed proforma, this pre-tax negative cash flow is $1,695 the first year, or about $141 per month. Negative cash flow should decrease as rents rise if operating expenses are controlled. (Negative cash flow in this case for the first year is the difference between net rental income ($5,700) and the operating expenses ($2,615, including real property taxes), principal payments ($240) and interest payments ($4,540)—see the proforma). Note that this sum ($1,695 the first year) comes out of your pocket. It is *not* the equivalent of a tax loss, which is comprised of components that are completely deductible. In this case, there is a tax loss (or write-off) of $7,575 in the first year and $5,720 in the second year. This is directly deductible from your other income, dollar for dollar, but the maximum benefit, after tax, is half that amount since the hypothetical taxpayer is in the 50% bracket. (See the proforma at the end of this Part for calculations of the tax write-off.)

Why does the aggressive posture appeal to many purchasers? In return for the pre-tax negative cash flow (which should be less as rents rise), as an aggressive purchaser, you can acquire more properties (all of which should be appreciating) with your available capital and, thus, build a larger net worth much quicker. Your return on investment may be very high because, for one thing, your initial investment is small. At the same time, you will be cutting your tax bill faster since you will have more dollar amounts of interest, property tax, depreciation, and operating expense deductions (and, thus, larger tax write-offs). In addition, you have spread your risk over several properties instead of concentrating it in one asset.

Do you have to take this approach? No. Alternatively, if you are more conservative by nature and wish to take a go-slow approach, that is fine too. After all, you have to be comfortable, mentally and financially, with your purchase program. The conservative posture would be to structure the transaction so that there is no negative cash flow (break-even) or where there is a positive cash flow. To do this, you will have to increase the amount of money placed as a down payment—possibly up to 25 to 30% of the purchase price instead of 20%. On a $60,000 house, this would amount to $15,000 to $18,000.

The mental peace derived and the avoidance of negative cash flow is offset by a reduction in your tax benefits (since deductions such as interest would be less), and offset by the lesser amount of property (and resulting appreciation) which could be purchased, as well as the receipt of a lower return on investment. In addition, you are expending additional dollars up front on the down payment instead of utilizing others' money (as if the loan included these additional amounts). This throws you right into the inflation trap. You are using expensive (today's) dollars to make the additional amount of the down payment, instead of increasingly cheaper dollars to pay off a large loan balance.

If the transaction is structured such that a *positive* cash flow results, you have more income, but you also have more tax—and the purpose of this program is thwarted. In addition, by placing all of this money into one property instead of several, you are increasing your exposure (or risk) to the variations of one particular market. Thus, my suggestion is that if you feel that you must be conservative, at least do not opt for positive cash flow. This would be desirable only if you were already in a very low tax bracket and, even then, you are receiving only ordinary income, which is fully taxable (after deductions) as opposed to capital gains. (More about this later.)

10

Management of the Property

Advantages of Professional Management

It would be very wise to engage a management company to manage your property for several reasons:

1. They are professionals in this area where most of us are not, and they can relieve you of this burden at a relatively minimal cost.
2. Their services are tax deductible (as an operating expense).
3. They act as an insulator between you and the tenant. (For example, you would not receive a phone call at 2 a.m. from a tenant whose air conditioning is not functioning.)
4. They will be much closer to the property (if you do not live in the immediate area) and, therefore, can respond quicker to any problems.
5. They may have connections with appliance dealers and other suppliers of goods used in the operation of the unit.
6. They can provide for periodic maintenance and inspection of the unit.
7. All necessary services regarding the unit can be available under one roof.

Disadvantages of Professional Management

At the same time, there are disadvantages in using a management company:

1. Their services represent an additional out-of-pocket expense.

2. No one will care for your best interest (in this case, your property) better than you would, and that includes your property manager. There are some, though, that love their work and are excellent.

3. It is somewhat difficult to locate a good property manager. Certified property managers (CPM's) are often better than others, due to their training and concentration in the management field.

4. Some property managers engage in illegal practices. For example, some have reported vacancies when none have existed and yet have pocketed the rent. In the case of the single-family house, these types of fraud are harder for a dishonest manager to complete, due to the fact that only one rental unit at a time is undertaken, the unit is highly visible, and the illegal profit motive is not as great as in the case of a multi-unit building. If your controls over the property manager are proper, this kind of activity can be eliminated. Also, to assist in reducing this problem, management employees should be required to be bonded.

The advantages do seem to outweigh the disadvantages if there are proper safeguards. If the property is located outside of your own geographic area you probably have little choice.

Duties of the Management Company

The management company should be carefully selected with the assistance of the qualified real estate agent/broker who is representing you in this purchase transaction. If the proper management company has been selected, your only real physical duty would be to pay the mortgage. The management company should be required by written contract to perform the following duties:

1. All leasing, renting, operating, and managing of the premises.

2. Rendering of a monthly statement of receipts, expenses, and charges and remitting to you the receipts less disbursements according to standard accounting principles. (Note: if the disbursements exceed the receipts, you will most likely be required to promptly pay this upon demand by the management company.)

3. Depositing of all receipts collected (less any proper deductions) in an operating checking account.

4. Holding of all security deposits for your benefit, if so desired.

5. Bonding of all employees of the management company who handle or are responsible for your funds.

6. All advertising of the unit.

7. Signing, renewing, or cancelling of leases.

8. Collecting of rents due.

9. Institution and prosecution of actions against tenants and settlement/compromise/release of said actions.

10. Evicting and recovering possession of the premises.

11. Making or causing to be made and supervising of all repairs/alterations, decorating, and purchases and supplies for the premises. (However, you should require that the management company secure your prior approval on matters exceeding $100, with the exception of emergencies or monthly/recurring operating charges to maintain services to tenants, as required by the lease.)

12. Hiring/firing and supervision of all labor and employees required for the operation and maintenance of the premises.

13. Making service contracts for electricity, gas, fuel, water, telephone, window cleaning, rubbish hauling, etc.—but insist that the obligation terminate with the termination of the management contract. In this manner, you have more protection when and if you terminate a management contract.

Management fees for the aforementioned work should not be unreasonable: in the case of our $60,000 house, there is a one-time set up fee ($75), a monthly fee ($25), and a leasing cost of half of one month's rent ($250). Note that other companies may charge more, sometimes approximating 10% per month of the lease price.

11

Tenants

The management company you engage will handle the leasing function among its other duties. They are professionals, and know the "tricks" of the trade. Therefore, I am not going to discuss the mechanics of their job (for example, what form of lease or rental agreement they will use). However, I think that as owner of the property and user of their services you should be aware of and at least discuss the following points with your management company.

The Rental Application Form

When searching for prospective tenants, you should always bear in mind one important thought: A vacancy is sheer ecstasy compared to a bad tenant. Bad tenants bring noise problems, destruction to your property, credit losses, delinquency problems, and other costs and hassles associated with dealing with such persons. This ultimately includes eviction if necessary. It isn't a fun process. You can avoid these problem tenants by use of a well designed rental application form and interview procedure and a tenant screening service.

The application form should include the following points.

1. The applicant's personal information:
   a. His/her full name.
   b. Social Security number.
   c. Birth date.
   d. Height and weight.
2. The applicant's driver's license number (and state).
3. The applicant's residential history:
   a. Current address.
   b. Previous addresses (go back five years, if possible).
      For each part, the applicant should include the length of occupancy, monthly rent (or mortgage payment), the payee of these amounts, and reason(s) for leaving these previous residences.
4. The applicant's employment history:
   a. Current employer.
   b. Former employers (go back five years, if possible).
      For each part, the applicant should indicate starting and ending dates, supervisor's name and title, position and type of work, monthly income, and reason(s) for leaving. You must realize that you can be misled very easily on this part of the form. When checking these employment sources, you (or your management company) should not call the listed supervisor by name. Instead call the personnel department and ask *them* to identify the supervisor and then talk to him or her. Otherwise, a friend could be covering up for this applicant and your purpose for this detailed form has been thwarted.
5. Financial information:
   a. Checking accounts.
   b. Savings accounts.
   c. Monthly expenses (without accounting for rent payment).
      The applicant should list all checking and savings account numbers and the addresses of each financial institution. As to the monthly expenses, the applicant should be able to list his monthly expense (food, transportation, clothing, etc.). Adding to this his potential

rent payment and comparing this to his monthly salary, you can also determine if this applicant is acceptable. If his monthly expenses almost approximate his income, watch out! As discussed later, his income should be three to four times his rent payment. To this criterion, you will have to determine what a comfortable cushion between monthly expenses and income should be. Naturally, the larger the better (in the event some financial disaster hits the potential tenant). A 20% cushion would appear to be satisfactory.

6. Other miscellaneous information: Some management company forms include provisions for additional information about the applicant. For example, the applicant is asked to provide names, addresses, and telephone numbers of persons to be contacted in the event of an emergency situation. Why ask this? Of course, if there is an emergency, these persons could be contacted. More importantly, from your standpoint, if a tenant skips out without paying the rent, you have a much better chance at tracking him down.

The application form should indicate which fees are refundable. For example, you will require a deposit with this application. Should you turn down an applicant, the fee is to be returned to said applicant.

The form should conclude with the signature of the applicant and the date. Note also that it would be wise to include a paragraph before the signature guaranteeing the accuracy of the information. This paragraph could be phrased:

> The undersigned warrants that the aforementioned information is true and understands that the landlord will rely on its accuracy in his decision regarding this application.

This will weed out a few more fakers, since they will not wish to be caught in their own fraudulent trap.

Tenant Screening

Use of this application by itself is insufficient. When a person applies for the rental unit, you (or your management company) should "interview" each adult tenant (with a separate application form). Since you or your management company will personally fill out the form with responses from the applicant, you or he will obtain several additional benefits over allowing the applicant to complete the form. First, all-important reactions to the questions can be observed. Second, all questions will be answered properly and legibly.

With all of this information, and a separately signed release form authorizing financial institutions, employers, landlords, and others to release the applicant's credit, employment or other information, you and/or your management company should be able to determine if this applicant should be accepted. Credit checks, phone calls, and letters will be necessary.

Independent tenant screening services are also available to help weed out potential problem tenants. Use of their services by landlords is growing rapidly. These services maintain records on a potential tenant's credit, eviction history (if any), and other pertinent data collected from previous landlords and/or court records. For a relatively modest fee, landlords have reported a significant reduction in the number of short-term evictions of renters who moved in and immediately failed to pay rent.

Problem Tenants

While you may think of a large apartment complex having more problems with tenants, remember this important fact: For each of your properties, you have a minimal number of tenants (1 to 4) and, if any of them creates trouble, you have a major disturbance to your cash flow or to your property interest. The large apartment complex owner, while concerned, is not going to lose sleep over one problem tenant. He will just go about rectifying the problem in a business-like manner. Of course, everyone can have a financial problem at some time in his or her life, and this includes you and your tenants.

If your tenant does fall into a financial crisis, see if you can work out a solution with him, possibly altering his payment schedule. Instead of paying on the first of the month, the tenant could pay on the 15th of the month until he regains his job. Be clear with the tenant that this is only temporary—in fact, set up a time limit for this to expire. (Actually, the lease should include a late penalty clause. You can always waive it, when warranted.) After all, you are subsidizing him for this period and, in the short run at least, you are being hurt. Your cash flow is interrupted or altered, causing you to have to use your own back-up funds to meet this negative cash flow situation. This compromising attitude usually will create a good atmosphere between the tenant and yourself, and the remainder of this relationship should be very pleasant.

Contrast this approach to a more radical one. If you insist on his making the payment on time as usual, knowing full well that this previously good-faith tenant has lost his job, you create a very bellicose atmosphere. His impression of you is close to the dirt you are standing on. Do you care? You had better, because in the long run this relationship is headed for trouble. The best thing that could happen is that he will leave. After that, it's all down hill. If you go about the eviction process, many days will elapse before this process is complete. You have lost additional rent besides the cost and hassle of the eviction. The tenant might even destroy part of your property in protest.

Tenant Rights

You should be aware that tenants have various rights that fall into four categories.

Discrimination

Federal law prohibits discrimination against any person due to race, color, religion, or national origin in the sale or rental of housing or residential lots, in advertising, in financing, and in provision of real estate brokerage services. However, this does not mean that everyone qualifies for your rental property. If his income, employment record, etc., do not meet requirements, he can be refused, and he should be told specifically that he is being refused for these reasons only. This avoids future charges of discrimination. In addition, these laws do not apply to owners of *three or fewer* single-family houses and small owner-occupied buildings. Note also that state or local laws can be much more restrictive than the federal law.

Minimum housing standards

State and local agencies have established minimum health and safety standards for residential property. These regulations cover areas such as plumbing/sanitary suitability, electrical requirements, etc. The U.S. Department of Housing and Urban Development also has these types of standards and they apply to properties constructed, sold, or rented through Government financed programs.

Law of contract

A lawyer is a handy guy to have around in this area. Contract law covers all sorts of tenant/landlord areas such as the lease/rental agreement, the eviction process, and other contracts between the parties. These laws are a combination of statutory and common law and differ significantly in various states. A sharp lawyer can insure that these contracts are written in such a way as to be fair to both parties, and yet provide for the most efficient route through the court system if that becomes necessary.

Rent control

These ordinances, in a nutshell, restrict rent increases, evictions, and other actions against tenants. Generally, they are not beneficial to the landlord in any way and areas with such laws should be avoided, as previously mentioned, even though these laws may not apply to single-family houses. And, as described earlier, rent control ruins an entire area.

Children and Other Critters

Should you really rent to families with children? Probably yes. At this time, there is a very extensive market for this category of household. The supply of housing available to meet this demand, however, has been severely restricted by those who seek to exclude children from their property. According to the U.S. Department of Housing and Urban Development, less than 25% of all rental housing nationwide is available to families with children without any restrictions, and 25% is entirely adult-only oriented. In the nation's largest metropolitan areas the situation is more severe. With this type of situation, the person who is able to rent to a family with children can probably rent the unit more easily, obtain a premium rent, and potentially have the same tenants for a long time. Many landlords have indicated that families have remained tenants in their houses through the childrens' high school years.

Offsetting the aforementioned is the claim that children destroy property much more quickly than other tenant groups. This is probably an over-generalization. After all, adult tenants often have wild parties and are involved in altercations. It is also claimed that children are noisier than other tenants. This is not necessarily the case. Stereos, televisions, motorcycles, and domestic quarrels can be much noisier.

If all of the other tenant information checks out, the issue boils down to checking out the family very closely. For example, if they maintain a neat present home and/or appearance, dress their children properly, and the children are well-behaved, this family could turn out to be the best tenants you could ever encounter. If you are still hesitant about potential damage to your property by the children, obtain a larger security deposit—say 1½ to 2 times your former amount. (You might want to consider charging a larger security deposit fee in all cases. Since many states/localities are considering legislation to make it illegal to discriminate against families with children, it would be wise to anticipate potential problem areas, despite the fact that these laws most likely would not apply to single-family rental units.)

As to four-legged creatures, even though I love animals, you should be very suspect of tenants with pets. You might permit a cat or a *small* house dog. If a prospective tenant owns a large dog and you wish to rent to that tenant insist (in writing—everything should be in writing) that the dog remain outside at all times. In any case where pets are allowed, you should raise the security deposit to provide extra insurance for your property interest. Even outdoors a large dog can ruin shrubs and lawns. Indoors, the damage may be irreversible—at least in the case of some odors.

Income and Employment

You might consider imposing a higher income to rent ratio for prospective tenants. Many landlords will require as low as a 3 to 1 ratio—that is, the tenant's monthly gross income should be at least three times the rent charged. You could insist on a 3½ to 1 or 4 to 1 ratio. However, remember, as with any restriction that you impose, you will be limiting your potential market of tenants. In this case, if you wish to charge $450 in rent and require a 3 to 1 ratio, the tenant would need a monthly gross income of $1,350 to qualify. If your ratio is 4 to 1, he needs a gross income of $1,800 per month. There are more people making $1,350 per month than $1,800 and, in addition, the higher income earners may have the ability to buy their own homes.

The tenant should be able to show stable employment for at least a year. Yet, be somewhat flexible here; corporate transferees, young professionals right out of college/service, and others will not fit your rule but may be excellent prospective tenants. Naturally, a management company will thoroughly investigate this area, as well as other banking references and credit checks. The specific landlord references given by the tenant are critical—try to get the tenant's *previous* landlord's recommendation. He has nothing to hide. On the other hand, his present landlord may want him out so badly that he'll say anything.

Number of Tenants, Roommates, and Young Adults

You should insist on a limitation of the number of people allowed to occupy the residence. A good rule of thumb is no more than two persons for each bedroom in the residence. As to the particular tenants, your best tenants (in terms of scarcity of problems) come from the following areas: corporate transferees, families (both young and retired), and couples. Singles/roommates, while in large part may be great tenants, often as a group cause more problems than others for a variety of reasons.

If you do find yourself in a situation of having to rent to roommates, you could make all sign the lease. Or, you could make one of the tenants fully responsible for all of the tenants. This may be a better technique, since this tenant will have to qualify on his income alone, which is a greater burden than if all were collectively responsible for the rent payments. Under no circumstances should a new roommate be allowed to substitute for another without your express approval.

You should be very careful in your consideration of the age of the tenant. It is a touchy area and, if not handled properly, may lead to a lawsuit. If you are concerned about a prospective tenant's age, especially in the case of a young person with little or no financial history to rely on, then insist that the parents or a legal guardian cosign the lease—making them also liable for rent payments and any damages.

The Move-In Inspection

You or your management company and your prospective tenant should together make a move-in inspection of your rental property prior to move-in. It should be done at this time to avoid damage by movers which the tenant will claim he did not cause or will hide. Otherwise, you may not be able to charge for these damages. The previous tenant is gone and you don't know who caused the damage. In fact, the lease should include this as one basis for the damages/security deposit clause.

To be sure, tenants are not required to pay for ordinary wear and tear on the property. But leases do make the tenant liable for damages in excess of these amounts. Security deposits are taken to cover such excess damage. However, this alone is no protection for you or your tenant. Without the move-in inspection, there is no conclusive proof that this tenant caused the damage. And, from the tenant's standpoint, he can't prove that he didn't cause the damage.

To rectify this, walk through the unit with the tenant before he moves in and after the previous tenant has moved out. In fact, this inspection can also serve as the *move-out* inspection for the previous tenant. All damages should be noted in writing. The form on which this is done should contain all pertinent data such as the tenant's name, address of the unit, the date, the areas inspected, and the defects. A clause should be included which testifies to the good condition of the unit other than the noted defects, that a complete inspection has been made by the tenant, and that the tenant assumes responsibility for any damage other than ordinary wear and tear. The document should be signed by the tenant(s), the landlord (or management company), and a witness if possible. The tenant should get a copy of this document. When the tenant moves out, repeat the same process with a new tenant. Compare the previous tenant's inspection with this new inspection. If the previous tenant has caused additional damage other than that noted, deduct the proper amount from the security deposit to cover the cost of those damages. If the damages are greater than the security deposit, bill the tenant for the extra amount.

Rent and Security Deposit

The rent you charge will depend to a great extent on market forces and the features of your unit. You should obtain the first and last month's rent upon signing the lease. Generally, these amounts are taxable for a cash basis taxpayer when received.

You should obtain a security/cleaning deposit of an amount equal to at least one month's rent—more if pets or other circumstances warrant it. This sum is generally not taxable to you as the landlord if it is a true security deposit. You have unrestricted use of these funds. If the security deposit can be applied by the landlord against final rental payments, it still may not be taxable *if* it is intended primarily to secure other lease obligations. (Proper intent must be shown.) To avoid any problems, it would be a good practice to stipulate in the lease that the security deposit may *not* be applied against the rental payments. This step will also make it less likely that a tenant will skip out without paying the last month's rent, leaving you with nothing for damages.

The Lease

You should use a standard form lease/rental agreement or one approved by the legal professionals in the area. If you need to modify the lease to meet your requirements (e. g., adding clauses such as those previously discussed in other sections of this chapter), do so with the aid of an attorney. The lease is your basis for controlling the property and the tenant while the unit is being rented. If the lease does not contain certain elements, does not conform to your requirements, or incorporates illegal clauses, your control is diminished. So, don't take chances with this document.

Basic Elements

A lease sets forth the rights and duties of both the landlord and tenant (aside from those relating to all real property—see "Tenant Rights," earlier in this chapter). The basic elements of a lease include the following:

1. *The parties.* They must be competent and under no duress to sign.

2. *A description of the leased premises.* This must be in some intelligible form—either street address and city or legal description.

3. *A demising clause.* This clause outlines that the landlord is leasing the aforementioned described premises to the tenant.

4. *The rent amount and receiver of such rent.* This section will include the rent amount, the frequency of rent payments, the date upon which the rent is due, and where and to what entity it is to be paid. *Note:* A kind gesture here (which doesn't cost you anything) would be to ask the prospective tenant when it is easiest for him to pay the rent, and incorporate this date into the lease. For example, if he gets paid on the 15th of the month, make that the rent due date. This will create good will with the tenant from the beginning.

5. *The starting date of the lease period and the duration of the lease.*

Additional Clauses

Additional clauses in the lease will set out your agreement as to rights and duties between the parties other than the basic right of possession in return for rent. These clauses will outline:

1. Whether utilities, appliances, garages, etc., go with the unit;

2. Whether the tenant may assign or sublet the space;

3. Whether children and/or pets are allowed;

4. Whether the tenant can make improvements or alter the property;

5. Whether the unit can be used for business purposes;

6. Whether the landlord can re-enter the unit for repairs or to show the unit to potential renters or buyers;

7. Your right to evict for certain nonperformance of the lease;

8. The tenants' remedy for interruption of his possession of the premises;

9. What happens if the tenant terminates the lease;

10. What happens if the landlord terminates the lease; and so on.

While all of the above clauses are critical, let me dwell on several at this point.

Inspection by Landlord. It is highly beneficial to be able to check on your property interest during the term of the lease. You want to make sure the property is being properly maintained and cared for. An outside inspection only reveals whether outside maintenance is being performed. But what about the inside of your house? Aside from an emergency, you have no way of knowing what is going on and no right to enter the premises unless some type of clause is included permitting you to do so. A good way to get around this, without alienating the tenant, is to provide for periodic furnace filter changes or other routine maintenance, to be performed "free" by you (or management company) at specified dates. At that time, you (or your agent) can visually inspect the inside without the tenant becoming overly suspicious.

Showing the House. Another clause is the re-entry clause for the purpose of showing the house to prospective tenants or buyers. In the case of re-renting the house, the lease should allow you (or your agent) to enter during daytime and early evening hours, say between 9 a.m. and 7 p.m., either by appointment or by key when the tenant is not at home. This gives you the maximum ability to re-rent the unit. Without this clause, you are at the mercy of the tenant and your property will likely be off the market more than it is on since the tenant will insist on all sort of restrictions to your access.

In the case where you believe you are going to sell the house, you should tell the prospective tenant before he moves in. The lease should outline his cooperation in the showing of the house—this is all important. Without this cooperation, a sale will be nearly impossible. Without it, when you do get access it will be at limited times or will be after the house is empty again. It is a proven fact that houses sell better, quicker, and for a higher price when they are occupied as opposed to being completely vacant.

Of course, you are reducing your prospective tenant market considerably in the beginning since not many persons want to completely move in only to move out within a short period. But, by telling the tenant and making this part of the lease, bad feelings are avoided and your property is less likely to be destroyed.

Early Termination. Another important clause concerns early termination of the lease. In this clause, you will outline specific terminating circumstances and ways in which you can effect an early termination. This clause will include the kind and type of notice to be given to the tenant, etc.

Subletting. You should insist in the lease that the tenant will not sublet the property or assign the lease to another without your express approval. This will give you the option of allowing another to take possession of the premises after he has been carefully screened. With a sublease or assignment, the original tenant should still be responsible for the rent, under one legal theory or another. So, your principal concern is the new tenant—are you going to have problems with him? If you know all about him in advance, you can save yourself potential future hassles.

Broken Leases. If the tenant wants to break the lease, you will have to weigh various factors. If he was a good tenant and is transferred by his company, let him out of the lease, as long as he has allowed you enough notice to get the property rented out. This way you can raise the rent to the next tenant and improve your cash flow at an earlier date. If he just vacates the property before the lease expires, he is still responsible for the rent due (and you will hold him responsible), although in some states the landlord must mitigate (take steps to lessen) his damages.

Vacancy Patterns

If you find, in your experience with this type of program, vacancy *consistently* above 5%, then you should do some investigating. You should start with previous tenants (assuming you know their whereabouts) and with a current tenant who has given notice. You personally (*not* the management company agent) should inquire as to why. Maybe the management company didn't treat him fairly. Maybe he is moving to a larger unit or is buying a house. Maybe he is being transferred to another area. Maybe you can persuade him to stay longer to give you time to find another renter. Offer him a break to stay. Maybe you can rectify the situation completely and keep a good tenant, even raising the rent if that is what is takes to fix a unit and if that is the problem. After all, the tenant will have to incur moving and other costs. If he is generally happy with the unit, he may stay if you can correct the problem.

If the tenant definitely is leaving for reasons such as transfer, etc. (unrelated to your operation), then don't waste a valuable source. Ask him if he can refer other potential tenants. Make it worth his while. If you accept one of his referrals, compensate him for his help. It is far cheaper, easier, and less time consuming to fill your houses in this manner. If the tenant has been a good one, his friends/referrals are more than likely to be also.

12

Operating Expenses and Other Considerations

Operating Expenses

Again, you should do your homework in choosing properties that are in good repair and relatively new. This will aid in minimizing operating costs. While operating expenses are deductible, they must still be paid. Therefore, you should be careful that they do not get out of hand. In the case of a single-family house, these expenses will be approximately 40 to 50% of gross income. In a multi-unit building, where some economies of scale are possible, the ratio would be closer to 35 to 45%.

Typical operating expenses include management fees, set up costs, cleaning, utilities, leasing costs, advertising, insurance, taxes, and repairs. For our $60,000 house, typical operating expenses for the first year approximate $2,615 (individual amounts can be seen by referring to the proforma).

Taxes

Note that real property taxes account for $1,400 of that amount and that, in Part III, I will list this expense separately in my examples. Regarding real property taxes, it may be possible to purchase two similar houses in two different areas with significantly different real property taxes. Choose the one you can live with financially. You already know that you can deduct these taxes, but again, if income from rentals does not cover all the expenses, you must be prepared to pay out of your pocket.

Repairs/Cleaning Expenses

I have deliberately listed "repairs" last because there is an important distinction to be made between repairs and capital improvements. A *repair* has been classified as something that does nothing more than keep the property in an operating condition over its probable life for the uses for which it was acquired. So, generally speaking, if you spend money for something that only serves to maintain value or the life of the property (example: fixing a hole in the roof of a rental building) then it is currently deductible. However, as a general rule, if the expenditure results in prolonging the life of the property or results in increasing its value (example: putting an entirely new roof on the rental building), it will be classified as a *capital improvement* which is *not* currently deductible but is added to basis and then recovered through depreciation deductions. (But note, there are grey areas.)

Repairs/cleaning expenses, more commonly referred to as maintenance expenses, will comprise approximately 5% of gross rental income. While many property managers utilize a 10% figure, this would be excessive for your program. A 10% figure would be reasonable for an abused building, but not a fairly new single-family house.

It is imperative that you do not defer maintenance on your property. This practice will hurt the property appeal to prospective renters. Further, lack of maintenance has a compounding effect, and in the long run will cost you much more, when major repairs are necessary.

Insurance

Ownership of rental property usually necessitates the purchase of various insurance coverages: fire, liability, workmen's compensation, theft, non-owned auto, etc. However, in the case of your investment in rental houses, more than likely you should only be concerned with variations of the first two types.

Property Insurance. You should undertake to insure your rental property from losses due to fire and other calamities as well as malicious mischief and vandalism (the mortgagee will insist on proof of certain coverages). Note that losses caused by smoke, water used to extinguish the fire, explosions during the fire, etc., which can be reasonably foreseen when a fire occurs, are covered—as long as other insurance clauses do not state to the contrary. You can also obtain extended coverage, which usually includes loss protection from damage caused by windstorms, hail, explosions, aircraft, vehicles, civil commotion, smoke, and so on. In addition, you should consider insuring the property against floods and earthquakes, if you choose to purchase property in areas that may be subject to these types of events.

The amount of property insurance coverage will be based on two factors: (1) the current cost of construction of your rental property, and (2) the coinsurance clause. You can obtain estimates of the value of the property from various sources: the mortgagee's appraisal made prior to the origination of the loan (although this value will include land value); valuation service companies such as Marshall & Stevens which prepare cost estimates of different types of construction in various locales; local builders and architects; and knowledgeable realtors in the area.

The coinsurance clause in the policy is a provision which prevents the insurance company from incurring loss liability in excess of the ratio of the insurance carried to the amount required. Generally, these clauses are written at 80 or 90%. Thus, you are agreeing to keep 80 or 90% of your property's value insured. For example, if the full value of your building is $50,000 you would have to insure it for $40,000. Thus if you suffered a $20,000 loss, the insurance company would be liable for the full amount, since you carried the proper amount of insurance:

$$\text{Insurance Company Liability} = \frac{\text{Amount of Insurance}}{\text{Amount of Insurance Required Per Policy}} \times \text{Actual loss}$$

$$= \frac{\$40,000}{\$40,000} \times \$20,000 = \underline{\$20,000}$$

Contrast this situation with one where you only kept 70% of the value insured:

$$\text{Insurance Company Liability} = \frac{\$35,000}{\$40,000} \times \$20,000 = \underline{\$17,500}$$

You would thus have to bear $2,500 of the loss out of your own pocket.

Note that when a loss occurs, the policy face value is similarly reduced by this amount. You will have to pay an additional premium to increase the amount of insurance to the full amount prior to the loss.

You can reduce the amount of the premium by raising the deductible amount (similar to the concept in auto insurance). Thus, assuming a $500 deductible amount, you would have to pay the first $500 in any loss covered by the insurance policy.

Since the value of construction constantly increases, you should review your policy periodically to insure that you are carrying the proper amount of insurance on the property. Note that you may want to insure the rental income of the building. This can be done by endorsement to the property insurance policy.

Liability Insurance. Liability insurance does not cover loss to the owner's property, but instead protects the owner from liability when third parties are injured on the owner's property. If the owner is deemed negligent in its protection of third parties, the liability owed by the owner hopefully will be covered by his liability insurance contract.

The owner does not owe *everyone* who enters onto his property a duty of care. For example, the owner generally owes no duty to an undiscovered trespasser. In fact, the owner's liability to a trespasser often is only for willful injuries inflicted by the owner on the trespasser.

The owner does owe a duty of ordinary care to protect and provide safe premises to *licensees*. A licensee is one who enters the property with permission (it may be implied, as in the case of a salesperson) of the owner for his own particular purpose (e.g., to promote a product). The owner owes the highest degree of care to *invitees*, those persons who have been invited onto the property by the owner or his agent primarily for the owner's purposes.

A liability policy will cover injuries (sickness, disease, and death resulting therefrom) to those to whom the owner is legally obligated. It also protects the owner by insuring damage to the property of the third party, including loss of use of the property resulting from an accident within the hazards stipulated by the policy.

You should obtain maximum liability insurance coverage. A $1,000,000 policy is not that much more expensive than a $100,000 policy, but in an era of large court awards, can you afford not to be protected? The coverages included in the policy should be discussed with a knowledgeable insurance agent. Apartment owners' associations are a good resource in this regard also. When you own several properties, you may consider switching to a blanket liability policy covering all of the properties.

Workmen's Compensation. Since you have contracted with an independent property management firm to operate your single-family rental properties, you will not need this type of coverage.

However, you should ascertain prior to entering into a management contract that the management firm does have this type of insurance and that its subcontractors carry this coverage.

Practical Suggestion

One last practical suggestion. You may want to include water and yard maintenance in operating expenses as extra insurance for the care of the landscape and grounds. (This depends on the tenant and the property involved.) As you can see from the proforma, the *tenant* pays all utilities. The "utilities" included in your operating expenses cover the vacancy periods and act as a reserve. This accounts for the low figure of $40 listed in the proforma.

Other Considerations

Checking Account

Normally, you should establish a checking account with a minimum balance—typically $200 to $300—to operate the property. From this account, repair bills, etc., will be paid. This checking account serves an additional purpose. It, along with the contract with the management company and the operating expenses, provides circumstantial evidence that you are operating a "trade or business" (the operation of rental properties) as characterized by the Internal Revenue Code, and that you have not purchased these houses primarily for realizing appreciation. As previously discussed, the "trade or business" designation may be critical to obtaining the maximum interest deduction, as well as obtaining capital gains/ordinary loss treatment upon sale. More about this in Part IV.

Locks

It would be advisable to have all outdoor locks on the property changed before the tenant takes possession of the property.

Will

As a sidelight, it may be necessary to amend your will to include specific disposition of this real property depending on various circumstances. Again, you should consult your own attorney for advice.

13

Interest and Casualty Loss Expenses

Interest

You can deduct *all* interest paid or accrued within the taxable year on indebtedness. However, there are several areas that must be noted. In the area of "investment interest," there is a strict limitation on deductibility. For an individual, the limit is $10,000 plus net investment income, plus allowable deductions from property subject to a net lease if such deductions exceed the rental income. Further, this limit may be increased by up to $15,000 for a 50% owner of an enterprise. *Investment interest* is that interest paid on indebtedness incurred to purchase (or carry) investment property. Further, *investment property* is property not held for use in a trade or business, but for profit or income. Stocks or bonds are examples.

Operation of rental real property would be classified as a "trade or business" within the meaning of the Internal Revenue Code. Thus, generally it would *not* be considered investment property for purposes of this investment interest discussion, and you can forget about this interest deduction limitation. But you should still make sure that you conduct your operations as a trade or business. That is, the circumstantial evidence I discuss in the Overview and later in this Part may be crucial should the IRS challenge you.

There are two exceptions to the general rule that operation of rental real property is a "trade or business." First, if the real property is unimproved property (land) then the IRS may feel that your activity in regard to said property is too meager to constitute a "trade or business" designation. Second, if you lease property on a "net basis," then this will not be treated as a trade or business. *Net basis* (for purposes of this section of the Code) means a situation where the owner's trade or business deductions (excluding tax, interest, and depreciation) are less than 15% of the rental income, or it is a situation where the lessor-owner is guaranteed a specific return on the investment, or a situation where he is guaranteed against loss.

These two exceptions should *not* apply if you purchase houses (or other improved property), lease the property out, and are responsible for the operating expenses (as in the proforma and in all examples in this discussion). In addition, you should conduct yourself in such a way that there is no question that this rental program is a "trade or business."

Points is a term often used to describe the charges paid by a borrower to the lender in addition to the rate of interest quoted on the loan. A *point* is one percentage point of interest (1%) of the loan amount and is payable in advance. Thus, in effect, the actual annual percentage rate (APR) of interest is higher and the net loan proceeds to you are lower.

Tax treatment of these points (often called "loan origination fees," "maximum loan charges," or "premium charges") depends on the type of property involved, the use of the loan proceeds, whether the charges are *solely* for the use of the money, and whether the points charged are for specific services by the lender for the borrower's account (such as the lender's appraisal fee).

If you obtain a loan to purchase or improve a house that is your personal residence and the loan is secured by this house, then the amount paid as points is immediately deductible in full in the year paid, if charging of these points in this amount is established business practice in your area and the amount charged does not exceed the amount generally charged. But, if the loan proceeds involved are used for other purposes, these points are treated as prepaid interest and must be amortized (spread) over the life of the loan. For example, if the points amount to $240, the loan term is 15 years, and the loan proceeds are to be used to put a new roof on your personal residence, then you can deduct the full $240 in that year. However, if you use the proceeds as a down payment on a house you will rent out to others, only one-fifteenth or $16 is deductible in each of the 15 years of the loan.

If the points are charged in connection with another loan, such as an equity loan on one of your rental houses, they must be amortized over the life of the loan.

If the points charged are *solely* for the use of the money, they are characterized as interest. If they are charged for specific services by the lender for the borrower's account, they are *not* interest.

Casualty Losses

As far as casualty loss deductions go, you should be aware that they are legitimate deductions. However, they do not occur on a regular basis. Any loss to property used in a trade or business caused by an external force, not under the control of the owner, which is not compensated for by insurance or its equivalent is deductible.

There are a few general rules to determine the proper casualty loss deduction. First, the measure of the loss is the difference between the fair market value of the property immediately before and after the casualty, but in no instance more than the owner's adjusted basis. The measure in some cases can be the cost of restoration. The amount of the loss deductible must be diminished by the amount of insurance proceeds (or equivalent) received by the owner. And, if the insurance proceeds paid to the owner exceed his adjusted basis, no deduction will be allowed.

14

Depreciation

The depreciation deduction is probably the most significant and, in some cases, the most complicated deduction to determine. (The proforma at the end of this Part outlines the depreciation deduction for purposes of this program.)

The Internal Revenue Code provides for a reasonable allowance for the exhaustion, wear and tear, and obsolescence of property used in a taypayer's trade or business, or of property held by the taxpayer for the production of income. However, land, being considered indestructible, is *not* depreciable. Therefore, this portion of the price paid must be excluded from any depreciation calculated. (The allocation on the property tax bill can be used to determine the proper portion to apply to the building and the land.)

The beauty of the depreciation deduction is that it is purely a *paper* deduction. You are not paying this amount out of your pocket to anyone. Compare this to the interest amount you pay to the bank, the real property taxes you pay to the governmental unit, and the operating expenses that are paid to various vendors. With depreciation, you receive the deduction and resulting tax benefits and still have the use of the deduction amounts *as well* as the amount of tax saved due to the deduction. As discussed later, when depreciation dollars are added back into income because of the lowering of basis, upon a sale it has been converted from ordinary income to capital gain and only 40% is taxable if the gain qualifies for long-term capital gains treatment. (If recapture applies, as discussed later, part of the depreciation deduction will be treated as ordinary income.)

With the passage of the Economic Recovery Tax Act of 1981, the Government has sharply limited the types of depreciation deductions permitted with regard to real property (effective January 1, 1981). In addition, the entire depreciation program has been revamped and is now referred to as the Accelerated Cost Recovery System (ACRS). Nevertheless, it is the same deduction. I prefer the term *depreciation*—it is shorter and most everyone has heard the term.

Under the new system, "recovery periods" are used to determine that time frame over which an asset can be depreciated. These time periods are shorter than the former "useful life" periods under the old law. *Useful life* was defined in the old law as that period over which the asset may reasonably be expected to be useful to the taxpayer in his trade or business or in the production of income. To illustrate the difference, under the new law, real property with a "useful life" of 25 years or less would have a "recovery period" of 10 years. Real property with a useful life longer than 25 years has a recovery period of 15 years.

For our purposes, the recovery period will be 15 years since the houses we are buying probably would have formerly had useful lives of 25 to 30 years. This represents quite a boon to persons owning rental property, as will be discussed further in this chapter. The IRS knows that and, remember, what the IRS giveth, it also taketh away. (Remember this line as you read the remainder of this chapter.)

Straight-Line Vs. Accelerated Depreciation

The two types of depreciation permitted are *straight-line* and *accelerated*. Let's study straight-line depreciation for a moment. Let's assume that you purchased a residential building on a piece of land for $140,000. The land is worth $40,000. (Salvage value at the end of the recovery period is ignored under the new law.) With straight-line depreciation, you could deduct the sum of $6,667 from your income. This figure is arrived at by taking the $100,000 cost basis of the building and dividing by the recovery period (15 years). (The straight-line rate is 6.67%: 100% ÷ 15 years.) Each year, as you take this deduction, you must adjust your basis by a similar amount. So, for example, in the first year, you would have had a

$6,667 depreciation deduction and your basis in the building at the end of the first year would then be $93,333; that is, the $100,000 you paid for the building part (your basis) less the $6,667 deduction. Basis is an important concept when you dispose of the property, and it is well defined in Part IV of this guide. Later, if you sell property you have depreciated on a straight-line program, the Government will recover the depreciation but only at capital gains rates, if you are careful. This is a key principle in tax shelter programs. More about this, too, in Part IV.

You can derive a larger depreciation deduction by using accelerated depreciation. For this type of real property, the IRS will now allow the use of a 175% declining balance method. This means that if the straight-line rate is 6.67% (100% divided by 15 year recovery period), the 175% declining balance method, *in theory*, will allow a 11.67% rate. This is an improvement over the former rule for *used* residential rental property. Before passage of the new Act (effective before January 1, 1981), you could use a 125% declining balance method with used residential rental property with a useful life of 20 years or more. However, in the case of *new* residential rental property, the 175% rate is inferior to the former rule. Formerly, you could take a 200% declining balance (two times the straight-line rate.)

Let's take the same property discussed earlier and see what the accelerated depreciation deduction would be. In the first year, we could take a deduction, *in theory*, of 11.67% of the building's value (1.75 times the straight-line rate of 6.67%). Thus, the deduction the first year would be $11,670. This amounts to a $5,003 greater deduction the first year using the accelerated instead of straight-line depreciation. As in the case of the straight-line depreciation, your basis must be adjusted yearly. So, after the first year, your new basis in the building would equal $88,330.

However, contrary to the straight-line system, you wouldn't deduct the same $11,670 amount each year. You remember that I called this the 175% *declining* balance system. That is, as the basis is adjusted each year, the deduction would decrease because you are applying the 11.67% rate to a smaller number. (Eventually, you will switch over to the straight-line system, because the straight-line deduction will exceed the accelerated depreciation deduction and, using this switchover to straight-line, the asset can be completely depreciated.

If you recall, I indicated previously that the 11.67% rate would, *in theory*, be applied to the declining basis figures. I want to take you

through an example so that you completely understand the accelerated depreciation concept, especially the declining balance method.
(Note that this example should not be relied upon for the accuracy
of the depreciation deduction amounts. The amounts shown will
not be those you would be entitled to deduct if, in reality, you
owned a $51,000 depreciable building. You will see why a little
later.) At this point, just understand the ideas involved. *Then,* I will
have a big surprise for you.

Assume that you buy a $60,000 house in Houston, Texas. What
would your depreciation deductions be over the 15 year recovery
period using accelerated depreciation versus straight-line depreciation? The land is worth 15% of the total price or $9,000. Therefore,
the building portion is valued at $51,000. The figures would look
like this:

Depreciation Deduction Schedule
Using Accelerated Vs. Straight-Line Depreciation
(Without Regard for Application of the Economic
Recovery Tax Act ACRS Percentages)

Year	175% Declining Balance		Straight-Line	
	Deduction	Basis at End of Year	Deduction	Basis at End of Year
1	$5,952	$45,048	$3,400	$47,600
2	5,257	39,791	3,400	44,200
3	4,644	35,147	3,400	40,800
4	4,102	31,045	3,400	37,400
5	3,623	27,422	3,400	34,000
6	3,200	24,222	3,400	30,600
7	2,827	21,395	3,400	27,200
8	2,497	18,898	3,400	23,800
9	2,205	16,693	3,400	20,400
10	1,948	14,745	3,400	17,000
11	1,721	13,024	3,400	13,600
12	1,520	11,504	3,400	10,200
13	1,343	10,161	3,400	6,800
14	1,186	8,975	3,400	3,400
15	1,047	7,928	3,400	—

Where you could have deducted $3,400 for each of the 15 years and
ended with a $0 basis ($3,400 × 15 = $51,000), instead you could
deduct $5,952 the first year, $5,257 the second, $4,644 the next,

and so on. But notice at the end of the 15 year period you would still own an asset that could have been depreciated another $7,928. If you were to abandon the property, you would take a loss in the last year, but this is not very likely since the asset is still very valuable. In fact, in 15 years this property could have an actual market value in the hundreds of thousands of dollars. You will also note that using the accelerated depreciation schedule, your deductions are less than the straight-line method after several years.

What do you do? You use a combination of both as shown in the following table. This is certainly permissible, although you would only take one kind of deduction in one year. Therefore, you would initially use the 175% accelerated depreciation method until the 8th year when you will switch to a straight-line method. This will ensure the maximum deductions and thus a depreciated zero basis at the end of the 15th year.

Depreciation Deduction Schedule with Crossover
(Without Regard for Application of the Economic
Recovery Tax Act ACRS Percentages)

Year	Deduction	Basis at End of Year
1	$5,952[a]	$45,048
2	5,957[a]	39,791
3	4,644[a]	35,147
4	4,102[a]	31,045
5	3,623[a]	27,422
6	3,200[a]	24,222
7	2,827[a]	21,395
8	2,674[b]	18,721
9	2,674[b]	16,047
10	2,674[b]	13,373
11	2,674[b]	10,699
12	2,674[b]	8,025
13	2,674[b]	5,351
14	2,674[b]	2,677
15	2,677[b]	—

[a]Accelerated depreciation (175% declining balance).
[b]Straight-line depreciation. Deduction in 15th year is slightly higher due to rounding.

Why do you switch at the end of the 8th year? Why not the 6th year, when the accelerated system would yield a deduction of

$3,200, which is smaller than the supposed straight-line deduction ($3,400)? Well, the key word in the previous sentence is *supposed*. Actually, the critical number to keep in mind is the basis figure. At the end of the 5th year, you would have a basis of $27,422. With 10 years of the recovery period remaining, you could go on a straight-line basis starting the 6th year and deduct $2,742 annually ($27,422 ÷ 10 years). So, the real straight-line deduction *is not* greater than the accelerated deduction amount at this time.

However, in the 8th year, the straight-line method *does* yield more benefit than the accelerated system. To determine this, look at the basis at the end of the 7th year: $21,395. Dividing this by the eight remaining years of the recovery period, an annual straight-line deduction of approximately $2,674 results. This exceeds the accelerated depreciation figure of $2,497 and those of later years. Therefore, for each year from the 8th year through the 15th, you would be deducting a straight-line amount of approximately $2,674.

ACRS Percentages

If you understand the theory, you are now ready for the surprise. The U.S. Treasury Department, in connection with the new Act, has devised a set of percentages to be applied to the original cost basis of the depreciable asset for each of the 15 years of the recovery period. These percentages vary in amount, according to the time the asset was placed into service. Thus, if you were to purchase a building and lease it to a tenant in January, it would generate the largest deduction (12%) and, conversely, if not placed into service until December, it would generate the least (1%). (Note that the 15 year recovery period could extend into the 16th *calendar* year if you placed the asset into service in March or later of the first year.

Table A on page 99 indicates the "Accelerated Cost Recovery Percentages" to be used under the 175% declining balance system.

For about the first seven years of the recovery period, the deductions allowed using the ACRS percentages approximate those you would have had with the 175% rate prior to implementation of the percentages (as in our theoretical example). The deductions resulting from both cases regarding our $60,000 house are shown in Table B. (Remember that our house was purchased and leased out in January of the first year.)

If you wish to use an accelerated depreciation method for an asset placed into service after December 31, 1980, use of the ACRS

TABLE A
ACRS Percentages Using the 175%
Declining Balance Method[a]

	Month Placed into Service in First Year											
Year	1	2	3	4	5	6	7	8	9	10	11	12
1	12	11	10	9	8	7	6	5	4	3	2	1
2	10	10	11	11	11	11	11	11	11	11	11	12
3	9	9	9	9	9	10	10	10	10	10	10	10
4	8	8	8	8	8	8	9	9	9	9	9	9
5	7	7	7	7	7	7	8	8	8	8	8	8
6	6	6	6	6	7	7	7	7	7	7	7	7
7	6	6	6	6	6	6	6	6	6	6	6	6
8	6	6	6	6	6	6	5	6	6	6	6	6
9	6	6	6	6	5	6	5	5	5	6	6	6
10	5	6	5	6	5	5	5	5	5	5	6	5
11	5	5	5	5	5	5	5	5	5	5	5	5
12	5	5	5	5	5	5	5	5	5	5	5	5
13	5	5	5	5	5	5	5	5	5	5	5	5
14	5	5	5	5	5	5	5	5	5	5	5	5
15	5	5	5	5	5	5	5	5	5	5	5	5
16	—	—	1	1	2	2	3	3	4	4	4	5

[a]Apply these percentages to the original cost basis. The switch from the 175% declining balance method to straight-line (at the appropriate time) has been incorporated into this table.

Table B
Depreciation Deduction Schedule
(Using the 175% Declining Balance Method)

	ACRS Percentages[a]		In Theory	
Year	Basis at Deduction	Basis at End of Year	Deduction	Basis at End of Year
1	$6,120	$44,880	$5,952	$45,048
2	5,100	39,780	5,257	39,791
3	4,590	35,190	4,644	35,147
4	4,080	31,110	4,102	31,045
5	3,570	27,540	3,623	27,422
6	3,060	24,480	3,200	24,222
7	3,060	21,420	2,827	21,395
8	3,060	18,360	2,497	18,898
9	3,060	15,300	2,205	16,693
10	2,550	12,750	1,948	14,745
11	2,550	10,000	1,721	13,024
12	2,550	7,650	1,520	11,504
13	2,550	5,100	1,343	10,161
14	2,550	2,550	1,186	8,975
15	2,550	—	1,047	7,928

[a]Crossover to straight-line depreciation has been incorporated into the ACRS percentages. It occurs here in the 10th year.

percentages is *mandatory*. This is both good news and bad news. Since I am an optimist, I will tell you the good news first. The task of actually determining the depreciation deduction has been greatly simplified. You apply the percentage for that year to the original cost basis and the result is your deduction amount. That's it. You do this each year. For example, in the first year in our example you would be able to deduct $6,120: 12% times the $51,000 original cost basis of the building. Of course, you will still annually adjust your basis by the depreciation amount. So, after the first year, your adjusted basis is $44,880: $51,000 less $6,120.

You no longer have to determine the crossover point where you switch from accelerated to straight-line depreciation. It has been determined for you in the percentage table. In our example, it occurs in the 10th year. Thus, for the $60,000 house ($51,000 building value) we have used as our example and, not coincidentally, also the typical house we will use for the discussion in this guide, the deductions will be as shown in the following table. (Note that you have fully depreciated the building at the end of the 15th year.)

Depreciation Deduction Schedule
with Crossover Under Economic Recovery Tax Act
of 1981[a]

Year	Deduction	Basis at End of Year
1	$6,120	$44,880
2	5,100	39,780
3	4,590	35,190
4	4,080	31,110
5	3,570	27,540
6	3,060	24,480
7	3,060	21,420
8	3,060	18,360
9	3,060	15,300
10	2,550	12,750
11	2,550	10,200
12	2,550	7,650
13	2,550	5,100
14	2,550	2,550
15	2,550	—

[a]Using ACRS percentages. These are the correct deduction amounts under the new Act.

On the other hand, the bad news is that since the application of these percentages is mandatory, this makes it easy for the IRS to check for variances in this area. Therefore, you must be careful to only deduct the amounts allowed. A more aggressive deduction approach is going to more than likely trigger an audit.

Now that you understand how accelerated depreciation works and realize that the 175% declining balance accelerated depreciation method yields larger depreciation deductions than straight-line for a certain length of time, you are probably wondering why everyone with rental property doesn't use this method. There are several answers. First, the smart money *does* use this method. The smart money recognizes the advantages of accelerated depreciation in spite of a few Internal Revenue Code sections that must be complied with. (These areas will be discussed shortly.) Second, the others are either scared or misinformed. This group feels that the IRS frowns on accelerated depreciation and instead, wants them to hold property for long periods using the straight-line rate. They don't. This group doesn't understand "recapture" and "add-on" minimum taxes for "preference" items. I will explain these terms. If my explanations do not satisfy you, please consult your tax lawyer or accountant. Finally, this group believes the additional calculations are too complex for them. I hope the aforementioned analysis disproves that.

Excess Depreciation

Recapture of Depreciation

Depreciation in excess of that determined under the straight-line method is taxable as ordinary income. For example, if you held the aforementioned $60,000 home for two years, you could have deducted, over those two years, depreciation amounts totaling either $11,220 (under the 175% declining balance method) or $6,800 (under the straight-line method). If you then sold the property for a gain and you had chosen the accelerated depreciation method, the difference ($4,420) would be taxable at *ordinary* tax rates. This is known as *recapture of depreciation.*

This is not as bad as it might initially appear. In effect, the Government has, for the two year period, made a loan to you tax-free of the excess amount. In that period, due to the higher depreciation deduction, you have had a smaller taxable income taxed at lower marginal rates. Also, the rates have been decreasing, due to the Economic Recovery Tax Act of 1981, which put you in even a lower tax bracket. You had the use of the deduction amount as well as the tax savings because of this deduction. Now, when you sell the property, the loan is coming due. But note, since you are in a much lower tax bracket now, your taxes on this amount are less than a similar amount of taxable income would have been two years earlier. Again, the Government is encouraging the development of more housing units. So take them up on their offer—benefit by it.

Add-On Minimum Tax

Another section of the Internal Revenue Code to be aware of when discussing accelerated depreciation is the "add-on" minimum tax. As previously discussed, excess depreciation is classified as a "tax preference" item. As such, this tax preference item is subject to an "add-on" minimum tax of 15% of the amount by which the tax preference item exceeds the *greater* of (a) $10,000 ($5,000 for a married person filing a separate return) or (b) an amount equal to one-half of the taxes imposed by the Internal Revenue Code (less certain credits). (The latter calculation is generally not important until the taxpayer has significant *taxable* income.)

In our case, excess depreciation totaled $4,420. Assume a couple, filing jointly, had a taxable income of $31,000. Since the excess depreciation tax preference item actually is less than $10,000, no "add-on" tax would have been imposed.

Component Depreciation

What the IRS giveth, it taketh away. Remember I said that? Well, they have done it again. Fortunately, it could have been worse. Before passage of the new tax Act, there was a hybrid type of depreciation system permitted called *component depreciation*.

The gist of component depreciation is that the various components of the structure (the basic structure, the ceiling, the floors and coverings, the plumbing, the wiring, etc.) comprise certain percentages of the total structure and each has a separate and different useful life. Thus, each component would be depreciated separately and the combination of all of these would yield the total depreciation deduction. The property owner could use either straight-line or accelerated depreciation rates within the component depreciation program. Thus, in most cases, the use of component depreciation provided the user with significantly higher deductions than normal straight-line or accelerated methods. The IRS didn't care for this system but tolerated it. The user had to obtain an independent appraisal regarding allocation of costs (based on value at acquisition of the property) and useful lives to the component parts. The IRS really objected to the use of this system with regard to used real property, although it grudgingly accepted the appraiser's report.

Using the former tax law and component depreciation (with an underlying straight-line rate), the same four-year-old $60,000 house discussed earlier could yield in each of the first two years $6,352 in depreciation deductions, none of which was recapturable or subject to additional taxes. The figures are shown below:

Component Depreciation[a]

Component	Percent	Remaining Life	Cost	Depreciation
Basic structure	20	26	$12,000	$ 462
Interior construction:				
Walls	15	10	9,000	900
Millwork	5	6	3,000	500
Floor & Covering:				
Carpet	3	2	1,800	900
Vinyl	1	2	600	300
Ceiling	2	14	1,200	86
Roof & Cover	8	10	4,800	480
Heating & Air				
Conditioning	7	4	4,200	1,050
Electrical	3	14	1,800	129
Plumbing	8	11	4,800	436
Appliances	2	3	1,200	400
Parking	8	10	4,800	480
Landscaping	2	11	1,200	109
Fence	1	5	600	120
TOTAL	85		$51,000	$6,352
LAND	15		$ 9,000	
TOTAL COST	100%		$60,000	

[a]Utilizing former tax law. Straight-line underlying rate. Four-year-old house in Houston, Texas. Building basis is $51,000. This depreciation method is no longer permitted on real property placed into service as of January 1, 1981.

To determine the depreciation amount for each component, you first would have determined the useful life of each and what percentage each component comprises of the total structure. The cost of each is determined. The cost is then divided by the useful life. For example, the basic structure has a remaining useful life of 26 years. It comprises 20% or $12,000 of the total value of the house. It contributes $12,000 divided by 26 years or $462 annually to the total depreciation deduction. The total depreciation deduction would diminish somewhat as the useful lives of each component were extinguished.

If a pure straight-line rate had been used under the old law, the maximum annual deduction would approximate $1,962 ($51,000 cost basis divided by the 26 year useful life, with no salvage value.) Thus, you could, by use of component over the straight-line, have had an additional $4,390 amount to deduct without recapture applying at the time of sale.

In light of the new Act, if component depreciation were available today, the amount of the depreciation deductions would be staggering, especially if accelerated rates were used. But it's not. However, note that the result of our 175% declining balance method almost approximates the deduction using the component depreciation method ($6,120 vs. $6,352) in the first year. And, note also that, in using the accelerated method, recapture and add-on taxes are not the obstacles many of you may have thought.

So we should be happy that the system is as good as it is, and thankful that there is such a deduction in the first place. And, it is clear that this deduction is vastly important to the taxpayer. It will not apply to any personal residence. And, as a further note, if you rent one of your depreciable rental properties to a relative, a bona fide lease must be executed and a fair market rent must be charged. Otherwise, the IRS may have a basis for questioning your deductions.

PROFORMA
(For a $60,000 Rental House in Houston, Texas)

SUMMARY

Cost of house	$60,000
Investment over a two year period	14,555
(Original cash down payment + 2 year's negative)	
Estimated write-off	(6,648)
Estimated return on investment after taxes for a two year period	88.24%

Comparison of rate of return on investment after taxes assuming the same investment is made in a Certificate of Deposit at 10% interest for a two year period.

Rate of return on Certificate of Deposit at 10% over two years after taxes	10.25%
Rate of return on proforma of average house	**88.24%**

Comparison of rate of return of the proforma of the average house over the rate of inflation

Rate of return after taxes on proforma of the average house	88.24%
Rate of inflation (assuming a 10% annual rate of inflation)	21.00%
Investor remains ahead of inflation	**67.24%**

Rate of return if investor disposes of property by a non-taxable (I.R.C. section 1031 exchange) sale

Estimated gain on disposition before taxes*	$12,208
Estimated tax savings	6,648
Total gain	$18,856
Rate of return	**129.55%**

---

*CAUTION: Taxes are deferred, not avoided.

Note: All four (4) pages are an integral part of the proforma.

INVESTMENT (Estimated holding period—two years)

Purchase price of average house		$ 60,000
Less: Down payment		(12,000)
Balance financed by assuming mortgage		$ 48,000
Monthly payment at 9¾% interest (10% APR) (principal, insurance, taxes and interest)	$ 540	

CASH OUTLAY

Down payment	$ 12,000	
Sustain negative cash flow year 1	1,695	
Sustain negative cash flow year 2	860	
Total cash invested		$ 14,555

CAPITAL APPRECIATION AND SALES PRICE

Purchase price		$ 60,000
First year appreciation—15% of $60,000	$ 9,000	9,000
Second year appreciation—15% of $69,000	10,350	10,350
Estimated capital appreciation	$ 19,350	
Estimated sales price		$ 79,350

COMPUTATION OF GAIN ON SALE

Estimated sales price		$ 79,350
Less: Commission	$ 4,761	
Other sales expenses	2,381	(7,142)
Estimated net sales price (Amount realized)		72,208
Less: Cost of house		(60,000)
Estimated gain on sale		$ 12,208

TAX ON GAIN ON SALE (Assuming no tax-free exchange)

Amount realized		$ 72,208
Less Adjusted basis		
Original basis (purchase price)	$ 60,000	
Less: Depreciation	(11,220)	(48,780)
Gain		$ 23,428
Less: Excess depreciation		(4,420)
Capital gain		$ 19,008
Taxable portion (40% of gain)		7,603
Plus: Ordinary income due to depreciation recapture		4,420
Total taxable gain		$ 12,023
Tax (50% tax rate; excludes state tax effects)		$ 6,012

COMPUTATION OF GAIN AFTER TAXES

Estimated gain on sale (above)		$ 12,208
Less: Estimated tax on gain		(6,012)
Estimated net gain after taxes		$ 6,196

ESTIMATED RETURN ON INVESTMENT AFTER TAXES

Tax savings on two years of tax write-off ($7,575 the first year and $5,720 the second, assuming a 50% tax rate)		$ 6,648
Estimated net gain after taxes		6,196
Total tax savings and gain after taxes		$ 12,844

RATE OF RETURN ON INVESTMENT AFTER TAXES   88.24%

ESTIMATED ANNUAL TAX WRITE-OFF		First Year		Second Year*
Rental income (12 months)		$ 6,000		$ 6,300
Less: Estimated vacancy—5%		(300)		—
Net rental income		$ 5,700		$ 6,300
Less: Operating expenses				
Management	$ 300		$ 300	
Set up cost	75		—	
Repairs, cleaning	250		300	
Utilities	40		60	
Leasing cost	250		—	
Advertising	25		—	
Insurance	275		320	
Taxes	1,400		1,400	
Total operating expenses		$ (2,615)		$ (2,380)
Net operating profit		$ 3,085		$ 3,920
Less: Interest	$4,540		$4,540	
Depreciation	6,120	$(10,660)	5,100	$ (9,640)
Estimated annual tax write-off		$ (7,575)		$ (5,720)

ESTIMATED ANNUAL PRE-TAX NEGATIVE CASH FLOW**				
Net rental income (above)		$ 5,700		$ 6,300
Less: Operating expense (above)	$2,615		$2,380	
Principal payments	240		240	
Interest payments**	4,540	7,395	4,540	(7,160)
Estimated annual negative cash flow†		$ (1,695)		$ (860)

ESTIMATED ANNUAL POSITIVE AFTER-TAX CASH FLOW‡			
Estimated pre-tax cash flow (above)		$ (1,695)	$ (860)
Plus: Tax shelter benefit (50%)		3,788	2,860
NET AFTER-TAX POSITIVE CASH FLOW		$ 2,093	$ 2,000

DEPRECIATION

Average Purchase Price	$60,000
Less: Estimated Land Value	(9,000)
Depreciable Basis (House in Texas)	$51,000

Using 175% declining balance (with switchover to straight-line in year 10). Recovery period is 15 years.

---

*Assume the same tenant. The rent has increased 5%. Vacancy is 0%.
**For purposes of this illustration, assume these payments remain constant. In reality, they would decrease only slightly over the first years.
†The investor that so desires may achieve a break-even or a positive cash flow by increasing the original investment.
‡Assumes the taxpayer-investor is in a 50% tax bracket. State tax effects have been excluded in these calculations.

Note: All four (4) pages are an integral part of this proforma.

Depreciation Deduction

Year	Amount	Basis at End of Year
1	$ 6,120	$44,880
2	5,100	39,780
3	4,590	35,190
4	4,080	31,110
5	3,570	27,540
6	3,060	24,480
7	3,060	21,420
8	3,060	18,360
9	3,060	15,300
10	2,550	12,750
11	2,550	10,200
12	2,550	7,650
13	2,550	5,160
14	2,550	2,550
15	2,550	—
Total Depreciation	$51,000	

In preparing the proforma, certain assumptions and estimates have been made. These are based on past experience, present conditions, and judgment. However, the investor should be aware that there is no guarantee that the operation of each individual property will result in the estimated proforma because it is predicated in part on future events that are not able to be predicted with absolute accuracy.

The proforma illustrates certain tax consequences which may or may not be applicable to each investor. (YOU ARE ADVISED TO CONFER WITH YOUR OWN TAX ATTORNEY.)

Note: All four (4) pages are an integral part of this proforma.

Part III

The Technique in Practice

15

Last Year—The Government Thanks You

Now that you have a general idea of what is involved, it is time to put the technique to the test. I've chosen a typical scenario as a base for our discussion.

You would have bought your first house for use as a personal residence four years ago. You and your spouse file a joint tax return, reporting a gross income of $35,000. Both of you are residents of California, are under 65 years of age, and have two minor children living at home. You and your spouse had monthly car, retailer, and other loan payments, of which the annual interest charges total $1,000. On last year's federal income tax form you claimed a total of $400 of medical, charity, and miscellaneous deductions. Real property taxes on your residence approximated $800. State/local taxes that year approached $938, and general sales taxes amounted to about $400. You claimed a deduction for your automobile licenses of $100. Interest (9¼% APR) on the house located in California totals about $4,700 per year. The mortgage balance at the end of last year approximated $52,000. The house was purchased for $67,000 and at year end was worth $140,000. You claimed all personal exemptions available to you. What did your federal income tax bill look like?

Federal Income Tax Liability Last Year
(with personal residence only)

Gross income/Adjusted gross income			$35,000
less personal exemptions			(4,000)
less itemized deductions			
medical, charity, misc.		$ 400	
taxes	$ 938		
state/local	800		
real property	400		
general sales	(N/A in CA)		
personal property	100		
other (car license)			
Subtotal		$ 2,238	
interest			
home mortgage	$4,700		
charge cards, car	1,000		
Subtotal		$ 5,700	
Total itemized deductions		$ 8,338	
less zero bracket amount		(3,400)	
Excess itemized deductions			(4,938)
Taxable income			$26,062
FEDERAL INCOME TAX[a]			$ 4,911

[a]Reflects Economic Recovery Tax Act of 1981 1.25% tax credit.

Thus, your federal income tax liability is $4,911 and you are in a 32% marginal tax bracket. That is, for every additional $1.00 more of ordinary income you will pay $0.32 in federal income taxes (until this additional income pushes you into an even *higher* bracket).

About the only thing you accomplished last year, aside from some relief afforded by ownership of your personal residence, was to give the federal and state governments more money to spend. If you're like most people, you need the money much more than they do. Besides, how much benefit do you directly or indirectly receive from various government spending programs? If you have a hard time answering that, let's attempt to do something about the situation.

16

Year 1—You've Decided to Fight Back

You have read the Overview and the first two Parts of this guide and have realized the potential of such a program. You have done your homework in analyzing markets and particular parcels of real property. You are at the point where you find a $60,000 house in Texas (as described and discussed in Part II) that you think might be a good rental house and that might give some tax relief. Should you buy it?

You determine that the house has a negative cash flow—$1,695 worth, as discussed in Part II. You are very concerned about the fact that money is going to come out of your own pocket to support this investment. This is a well-intentioned, but misplaced concern. You are looking at the wrong indicator. You have been looking at pre-tax cash flow. It is *after-tax* cash flow that is critical. If the after-tax flow is positive, or even near break-even, you would generally invest in such an opportunity. In this case, the figures reveal the following:

Estimated pre-tax negative cash flow	$(1,695)
Plus: Tax shelter benefit (@ 32% marginal rate)	2,424
After-tax cash flow	$ 729

Since the after tax cash flow is positive, you would want to make this investment (all things being equal).

In light of the aforementioned, you purchase the residence effective January 1, this year, using your savings for the down payment. You engage a good management company and, effective January 19, your first tenant moves in and takes possession (5% vacancy factor utilized). The net rental income is $5,700. The deductions associated with this property are those noted in previous Parts and, in particular, the proforma in Part II: $1,400 for real property taxes, $4,540 for interest, $6,120 for depreciation, and $1,215 for other operating expenses. Your personal exemptions are the same. Assume that your itemized deductions remain the same except that state/local taxes will now be about $589, general sales taxes about $470, and medical, charity, and miscellaneous deductions of $600. Assume that your wage income has risen 7% to $37,450. One year later, what does your federal income tax liability look like? (Assume that the tax laws do not drastically change with the exception of the addition of the various provisions of the Economic Recovery Tax Act of 1981, which take effect at different intervals.)

Note that the Economic Recovery Tax Act of 1981 provided for marginal tax bracket reductions through 1984. In year 1, after investment in one rental house, your marginal rate would have been 28% if the Act had not been passed. Under the Act, your true rate is 25%, or three percentage points less. Under the new Act, had it existed previously, you would have been in a 29% bracket prior to the initiation of this program, and not in the 32% bracket.

Also note that the Act provided for "marriage penalty relief" for two wage-earner married households. On 1982 returns, the lesser earning spouse can deduct up to 5% ($1,500 maximum) of his or her earnings from gross income on a joint return. In 1983, and subsequent years, this deduction increases to 10% ($3,000 maximum). For the sake of simplicity, this "marriage penalty relief"was not used in any tax calculation in this guide.

Your federal income taxes are now approximately $3,141 and you are now in the 25% (28% without the new Act) marginal bracket. Your taxes are only 64% of what they were when you only owned your personal residence and your income was $35,000. However, your total income has risen $8,150, or 23.3%, and in addition, you have the paper deduction (depreciation) amount of $6,120 available to spend. After-tax spendable income (gross income plus depreciation, less: trade or business expenses, itemized deductions, federal taxes, all principal payments, and points in the year loan is made) has increased a total of $2,604, or 14.2%, over the previous year. Incidentally, while this guide does not focus on state (California)

Federal Income Tax Liability for Year 1[a]
(with personal residence and one rental house)

Gross Income[b]			$43,150
less "trade and business" expenses (Texas property)			
real property taxes	$1,400		
interest[c]	4,540		
depreciation	6,120		
other operating expenses	1,215		
Subtotal			(13,275)
Adjusted gross income			$29,875
less personal exemptions			(4,000)
less itemized deductions			
medical, charity, misc.		$ 600	
taxes			
state/local	$ 589		
real property	800		
general sales	470		
personal property	(N/A in CA)		
other (car license)	100		
Subtotal		$ 1,959	
interest			
personal residence	$4,700		
charge card, car	1,000		
Subtotal		$ 5,700	
Total itemized deductions		$ 8,259	
less zero bracket amount		(3,400)	
Excess itemized deductions			(4,859)
Taxable income			$21,016
FEDERAL INCOME TAX[d]			**$ 3,141**

[a]The above calculations assume that you have not borrowed the amount necessary for the down payment. However, if you had, the effect would be to lower your taxable income (since the additional interest is deductible) and thus your taxes would be lower.
[b]Wages $37,450; net rental income $5,700.
[c]$48,000 mortgage balance at 9¾% interest (10% APR).
[d]Reflects Economic Recovery Tax Act of 1981 marginal tax rate reductions.

income taxes, in this instance they decreased by $349, or 37.2%.

What if your salary had increased by the 7% figure to $37,450, but you had not bought any income-producing rental property and you only owned your personal residence? (Assume all the same itemized deductions as above, except for state/local taxes which would approximate $1,098, an increase of about $160.) In that case, your federal income taxes would have risen from $5,047 to $5,911 (about 60.7% above their current level), even though your gross income would be $5,700 less. And you would have been in a 29% bracket (32% prior to the Act). By purchasing *one* $60,000 house used as a rental property the federal tax savings alone approaches $1,906.

You do have a pre-tax negative cash flow of $1,695, but this is covered by the federal tax savings ($1,906) and state tax savings ($509), and you still have $720 left to spend as you wish.

17

Year 2—April 15 Is Getting Less Painful

You are now beginning the second year of your acquisition program. Your wage income would again have risen by 7% to $40,072 and both your personal residence and the rental property would have appreciated greatly. Thus, at the beginning of Year 2, your personal residence should be worth about $150,000 and the rental property about $69,000. Both would have risen approximately 15% to reflect the sunbelt states' growth pattern. You have a good tenant in your first rental property who remains your tenant this year, with a 5% increase in rent to $525 per month (to match the market). However, you will get a full 12 month's rent, since there is no vacancy during this period. Therefore, you pick up this extra ½ month's rent. Furthermore, some of your operating expenses are eliminated: the leasing cost ($250), the set-up cost ($75), and the advertising expense ($25). Some of the operating costs in this typical $60,000 unit have risen: repairs/cleaning is now $300 instead of $250; the utilities cost has risen from $40 to $60; and the insurance cost has risen from $275 to $320. However, the depreciation deduction has decreased to $5,100.

The net result is to somewhat lower the annual tax write-off on this first unit from $7,575 to $5,720. In addition, offsetting the reduction in tax write-off, negative cash flow (out-of-pocket expense) on the first income property which you purchased should decrease to $860 (a reduction of $835). (Please see the proforma, Part II.)

You find a second $60,000 house in another area of Houston, Texas, for use as an income-producing rental unit. You would take title on January 1. The rent is up this year in the area of $525 per month (a 5% increase over last year). The same management company would be engaged and the tenant would take possession on January 19 (a 5% vacancy factor that amounts to $315). Your operating expenses for this second unit would be the following:

Expense	
Management	$ 300
Set-up cost	80
Repairs, cleaning	300
Utilities	60
Leasing cost	263
Advertising	35
Insurance	320
Taxes (real property)	1,400
Total	$2,758

Interest expense on the first mortgage would be the same, since I will asume for ease of discussion that you found another four-year-old house with an assumable 9¾% (10% APR) mortgage (balance of $48,000). The depreciation deduction should again approximate $6,120. Thus, the estimated tax write-off for this second unit in Year 2 is calculated as follows:

Rental Income (12 months at $525)		$ 6,300
Less: Estimated vacancy—5%		(315)
Net rental income		$ 5,985
Less: Operating expenses		$(2,758)
Net operating profit		$ 3,227
Less: Interest	$4,540	
Depreciation	6,120	(10,660)
Estimated tax write-off		$(7,433)

The estimated pre-tax negative cash flow for Year 2 on this second unit is determined as follows:

Net rental income		$ 5,985
Less: Operating expenses	$2,758	
Principal payments	240	
Interest payments	4,540	(7,538)
Estimated pre-tax negative cash flow		$(1,553)

Should you buy the second house? What is its after-tax cash flow? Both questions are answered by the following:

Estimated pre-tax cash flow	$(1,553)
Plus: Tax shelter benefit (@25%	
marginal rate)	1,858
After-tax cash flow[a]	$ 305

[a]Assuming the down payment is obtained without loan costs.

Since the after-tax flow is again positive, you would do well to consider the investment. Assume a tight money market exists—as often has been the case recently. To raise the down payment you decide to borrow on the equity of your personal residence, since you have determined that refinancing to raise the old loan amount and the down payment of $12,000 would be more expensive and that you do not have $12,000 in savings.

An equity loan of $12,000 for 15 years at a 15¾% APR of interest would cost you approximately $174.16 per month, $107.49 of which is deductible interest. You would have been charged probably two points (2% of the loan amount) to be treated as $240 of prepaid interest, which is amortized over the 15 year term. Thus, deductible interest in Year 2 is $1,290 annual interest plus ¹⁄₁₅ of the $240 worth of prepaid interest (or $16) for a total of $1,306. Refinancing the present $52,000 balance plus the $12,000 down payment would cost, at 13¼% APR for 30 years, $720.51 per month alone, without regard for other charges. In contrast, the total monthly payment of the old loan ($427.80) and the equity loan ($174.16) amounts to $601.96.

The beauty of obtaining the down payment in this manner is that property is, in effect, being 100% financed. Also, the loan proceeds come to you tax-free. None of your liquid assets are being used to purchase the property. This allows you to utilize your funds for other purposes and you have found a use for otherwise idle funds (the equity in your personal residence). Also, remember that you are using inflation to *your benefit* in three basic ways:

1. You are repaying all the indebtedness with dollars with increasingly less value (cheap dollars).
2. You are benefitting from inflation's effect in the appreciation of the properties you own.
3. The money you now have available from tax savings due to depreciation and other deductions can be invested in additional ways that either keep up with or exceed inflation.

What will your tax bill look like at the end of Year 2? Let's go through the calculations again. Note itemized deductions are the same except that medical, charity, and miscellaneous have risen to $800 (from $600), state/local taxes have decreased from $589 to $353, and the general sales tax deduction has risen from $470 to $500.

The federal income taxes now owing are only $1,990, only 40.5% of what they were when you only owned a personal residence and your income was $35,000. That is, the taxes this year are $2,921, or 59.5% less. You are now in a 19% marginal tax bracket. State taxes are $585 ($938 − $353) less. Yet, while your taxes are decreasing since you started the program of purchasing these houses and renting them out, your gross income has risen by $17,357, or 49.6%, and spendable income by $3,335, or 18.1%.

If you had not operated the two properties, your federal income taxes would have been nearly $5,149 this year—$3,159, or 158.7%, above the current level—despite the fact that your gross income would have been $12,285 *less*. Also note that state taxes would be $936 more than their current level.

This total tax savings of $4,095 offsets the pre-tax negative cash flow generated by the two properties (House #1: $860; House #2: $1,553), as well as most of the $2,330 in additional interest and principal paid on the equity loan. As you can see, without the equity loan you would be pocketing $1,682. However, by using your own cash for the down payment on House #2, you would be foregoing potential gains in other high-yielding investments or business opportunities.

You have been using the aggressive posture in investing in each individual property, but keeping your purchases to one house per year. The truly aggressive buyer would speed this up, as his finances

Federal Income Tax Liability for Year 2[a]
(with personal residence and two rental houses)

Gross Income[b]		$52,357
less "trade or business" expenses (Texas properties)		
real property taxes	$2,800	
interest	9,080	
depreciation	11,220	
other operating exp.[c]	2,338	
Subtotal		(25,438)
Adjusted gross income		$26,919
less personal exemptions		(4,000)
less itemized deductions		
medical, charity, misc.		$ 800
taxes		
state/local	$ 353	
real property	800	
general sales	500	
personal property	(N/A in CA)	
other (car lic.)	100	
Subtotal		$ 1,753
interest		
First mortgage	$4,700	
Equity loan[d]	1,306	
Charge cards, car	1,000	
Subtotal		$ 7,006
Total itemized deductions		$ 9,559
less zero bracket amount		(3,400)
Excess itemized deductions		(6,159)
Taxable income		$16,760
FEDERAL INCOME TAX[e]		$ 1,990

[a]The above calculation assumes that the down payment for rental house #2 has been borrowed.
[b]Wages $40,072; net rental income from house #1: $6,300; net rental income from house #2: $5,985.
[c]House #1: $980; House #2: $1,358.
[d]Annual interest of $1,290, plus prepaid interest (amortized points) in first year of loan: $16.
[e]Reflects Economic Recovery Act of 1981 marginal tax rate reductions.

permitted, but for the purpose of the discussion, our one-house-per-year plan will continue to be used. Using this approach in this guide will allow you to see the effect of each additional house on your taxes.

18

Year 3—Let's Do It One More Time

Again you find another $60,000 house in the Houston area. The negative cash flow is $1,118 and the tax benefit (@ 19% marginal bracket) is $1,330, for an after-tax cash flow of $212 (assuming a down payment free of loan costs). So, being the adventuresome sort, you go ahead and buy the house. Now you will have three rental houses. Let's go through the exercise just one more time—I *promise* this is the last time.

Assume your wage income has increased by 7% to $42,877. All rents have increased by approximately 10%. The renter in House #1 moves out and is replaced after a short (5%) vacancy period by another tenant. The renter in House #2 is a good tenant and decides to stay. House #3 (also four years old) is purchased for $60,000 in the Houston, Texas, area so that title passes January 1, and is vacant for 5% of the year before a tenant is found. The depreciation deduction in House #1 drops 10% to $4,590 (see Chapter 14) while the depreciation deductions in House #2, and House #3 should approximate $5,100 and $6,120, respectively. The interest deduction on the first mortgage is assumed to remain constant and the same for all three properties ($4,540 each). The down payment is raised through an equity loan on House #1. The equity in that house would be approaching $32,000, and, since a lender will generally loan up to 80% of the value, there should not be a major problem obtaining $12,000. The terms of the loan are, assuming a little bit easier credit period, 13¼% APR for 15 years. The monthly payment of $151.83 is comprised of principal ($66.67) and deductible interest ($85.16). The loan would be subject to two points (treated as $240 of prepaid interest—which again must be amortized) for a first year total interest deduction of about $1,038 ($1,022 in total annual interest and $16 in prepaid interest). The itemized deductions are as they appear in the tax calculation.

Operating expenses for the three units are as shown below:

Expense	House #1	House #2	House #3
Management	$ 360	$ 360	$ 360
Set up cost	—	—	85
Repairs, cleaning	350	350	350
Utilities	90	90	90
Leasing cost	288	—	288
Advertising	40	—	40
Insurance	340	340	340
Taxes (real property)	1,400	1,400	1,400
Totals	$2,868	$2,540	$2,953

The 1984 estimated tax write-off for each unit in year 3 is as follows:

Estimated Tax Write-Off (Year 3)	House #1	House #2	House #3
Rental income (12 months at $575)	$ 6,930	$ 6,930	$ 6,930
Less: Estimated vacancy—5%	(315)	—	(315)
Net rental income	$ 6,615	$ 6,903	$ 6,615
Less: Operating expenses	(2,868)	(2,540)	(2,953)
Net Operating profit	$ 3,747	$ 4,390	$ 3,662
Less: Interest[a]	$ (5,578)	$ (4,540)	$ (4,540)
Depreciation[b]	(4,590)	(5,100)	(6,120)
Estimated tax write-off	$ (6,421)	$ (5,250)	$ (6,998)
Plus: Interest payments on equity loan on personal residence[c]	(1,306)		
Total estimated tax write-off	$(19,975)		

[a]Re house #1: includes $1,022 yearly interest plus $16 prepaid interest (amortized points), in addition to the $4,540 on the assumed mortgage.
[b]Depreciation deductions decrease as time passes, in light of the method used.
[c]Includes $16 prepaid interest (amortized points).

The estimated pre-tax negative cash flow for year 3 on each unit is determined below:

Estimated Pre-Tax Negative Cash Flow (Year 3)	House #1	House #2	House #3
Net Rental Income	$ 6,615	$ 6,930	$ 6,615
Less: Operating expenses	(2,868)	(2,540)	(2,953)
Principal payments[a]	(1,040)	(240)	(240)
Interest payments[b]	(5,802)	(4,540)	(4,540)
Estimated negative cash flow	$(3,095)	$(390)	$(1,118)
Total negative cash flow (above)	$(4,603)		
Plus: Principal & Interest payments on equity loan on personal residence	(2,090)		
Total out of pocket expense	$(6,690)		

[a]Re house #1: includes principal payments of $800, due to equity loan on house #1.
[b]Includes $1,022 yearly interest plus $240 in points (actually prepaid) in addition to the $4,540 on the assumed mortgage.

The tax bill for year 3 will be determined by the calculations in the table on page 125. (Assume no significant changes in the tax laws.)

Federal income taxes are now $1,409, only 28.7% of the $4,911 in taxes that you owed the U.S. Government when you only owned your personal residence, earned $35,000, and had not started on your acquisition program. You are now in an 16% bracket as opposed to 32%. Your state taxes are only $229, or 24.4%, of the $938 at the time. And yet, your gross income has risen by 77.4%, or $28,037, to a total of $63,037, and your spendable income has increased to $23,036—a 25.3% (or $4,645) leap over that before you began to buy your rental houses.

Go back to our other benchmark—your tax position had you not purchased any income properties. Assume that your wages had risen by 7% per year for each of three years to a total of $42,877. Your federal income tax liability would then have been approximately $5,550, and you would have been in a 28% bracket (under the Act). Your state taxes would have been about $1,511. By purchasing these three income properties, you have saved $4,141 in federal income taxes ($5,550 − $1,409) and $1,282 in state income taxes ($1,511 − $229) in year 3.

These tax savings are offset by the out-of-pocket expenses: negative cash flow ($4,603) and monthly payments (year total) on the equity loan on the residence ($2,090). Thus, a shortfall between

Federal Income Tax Liability for Year 3[a]
(with personal residence and three rental houses)

Gross income[b]		$ 63,037
less "trade or business" expenses (Texas properties)[c]		
real property taxes	$ 4,200	
interest	14,658	
depreciation	15,810	
other operating expenses	4,161	
Subtotal		(38,829)
Adjusted gross income		$ 24,208
less personal exemptions		(4,000)
less itemized deductions		
medical, charity, misc.	$ 1,000	
taxes		
state/local	$ 229	
real property	800	
general sales	550	
personal property	(N/A in CA)	
other (car lic.)	100	
Subtotal	$ 1,679	
interest		
first mortgage	$ 4,700	
equity loan[d]	1,306	
charge cards, car	1,000	
Subtotal	$ 7,006	
Total itemized deductions	$ 9,685	
less zero bracket amount	(3,400)	
Excess itemized deductions		(6,285)
Taxable income		$ 13,923
FEDERAL INCOME TAX[e]		$ 1,409

[a]Assumes the down payment for both house #1 and house #2 have been borrowed.
[b]Wages $42,877; net rental income from house #1: $6,615; net rental income from house #2: $6,930; net rental income from house #3: $6,615.
[c]See previous pages, this chapter.
[d]$1,290 annual interest plus amortization of points ($16).
[e]Reflects Economic Recovery Tax Act of 1981 marginal tax rate reductions.

taxes saved ($5,423) and out-of-pocket expenses ($6,693) totals $1,270. Note that the taxes saved do cover the negative cash flow. As to other out-of-pocket expenses, a different form of financing of the down payment could reduce or eliminate any other expenses of this type.

You have available to you $15,810 of the paper deduction, depreciation. That is, $15,810 of your income is completely sheltered from taxation aside from the income sheltered by other deductions.

19

Performance Review

It would be advisable to assess your financial position after acquiring these three houses. In that regard, the following tables indicate some surprising statistics.

As one can see from the Income Statistics table, not only does gross income rise substantially when you use the program (or technique), but your spendable income also rises. It is true that spendable income is somewhat less than that without the program, but this is a reflection of the type and cost of financing used for the down payment. Remember, in years 2 and 3, equity loans were used. Of course, spendable income figures will vary anyway because each taxpayer's itemized deductions, etc., are different. And, with an average inflation rate projected by some at 10% per year, if increases in spendable income were the only measure of success, one would not undertake this program. But as discussed previously, and as will be discussed in later pages, there are many other benefits.

By using this program, in three years, after the acquisition of three houses and their subsequent rental, you have eliminated a full 60.7% of your income (federal and state) tax liability. Instead of paying $19,644 over the three years (years 1 through 3) you pay only $7,711, for a savings of $11,933. And, these are after-tax dollars saved, so the savings in income sheltered are actually greater than $11,933. You have offset *all* rental income plus, just due to the ownership of the three rental houses (without other itemized

Income Statistics

Year End	Gross Income[a]		Increase With Program		After-Tax Spendable Income[b]		Increase With Program			
	Without Program	With Program	Amount	Percent	Without Program	With Program	Amount	Percent	Amount Over Past	Percent
Pre-Program	$ 35,000	—	—	—	$ 18,391	—	—	—	—	—
Year 1	$ 37,450	$ 43,150	$ 5,700	15.2	$ 20,275	$ 20,995	$ 720	3.6	—	—
Year 2	$ 40,072	$ 52,357	$ 12,285	30.7	$ 22,374	$ 21,726[c]	(648)	(2.9)	$ 731	3.5
Year 3	$ 42,877	$ 63,037	$ 20,160	47.0	$ 24,306	$ 23,036[c]	(1,270)	(5.2)	1,310	6.0
Totals			$ 38,145	101.9			$ (1,198)	(5.9)		

[a]Wages in either case are assumed to increase by 7% annually.

[b]After-tax spendable income = gross income plus depreciation less: "trade or business" expenses (if applicable), itemized deductions (total), federal income taxes, principal payments (personal residence principal payments on first mortgage: $360 annually; other loans—car, charge cards, school, etc.: $3,000 annually), and full amount of points in year loan. Therefore, there would be a positive adjustment of $16 in Year 2 and $32 in Year 3, and this is reflected above.

[c]This figure could be higher under many circumstances. For example, you could have used alternative methods to obtain the downpayment—maybe an interest-free loan from a relative. In that case, in Year 3 the after-tax spendable income would increase to $24,897, despite the fact that federal income taxes and state income taxes are slightly higher at $1,568 and $271, respectively. Interest and principal expenses would decrease by $2,062. The increase then, in spendable income in Year 3 utilizing the program (over not utilizing it) would approximate $591, or 2.4%. Similarly, in Year 2, the spendable income could be greater.

deductions and personal exemptions), you have received $40,703 of tax write-off in three years' time.

The total depreciation (which accounts for part of the tax write-offs) for the three years totals $33,150. As previously mentioned, this is completely tax sheltered income, since it represents only a paper deduction. Of course, as discussed in Chapter 14, part of this depreciation, because the accelerated depreciation method was used, is subject to recapture as ordinary income. While this is something of which to be aware, as detailed in Chapter 14, you very well could find that the recapture provisions of the Code cause you very little problem at all.

The depreciation deductions in our program decrease over time (until the 10th year where the straight-line switchover occurs). This is due to the declining balance feature of the accelerated depreciation method used. However, significantly larger depreciation deductions are obtained over the straight-line rate in the first years of ownership. At a certain point, the particular house will be disposed of, since larger tax shelters and other tax benefits can be derived elsewhere.

Pre-tax negative cash flows and out-of-pocket expenses are significant but reasonable, in light of the aggressive acquisition posture. Since spendable income increases each year in spite of these out-of-pocket expenses, the concern should not be that this type of expense is a terrible thing to have, but that it remain within limits and does not increase too much in one year.

After seeing how gross income and spendable income rise while income taxes decrease, now it is seen that you have an asset build-up in real estate of $437,317; $239,603 or 121.2% higher than if you had never purchased any real property except your personal residence. (See the "Property Values" table on page 129.)

Further, the equity or that amount after indebtedness is subtracted (your net worth in these properties) approaches $222,237; $75,443 *more* than if no program had been undertaken. (Note as per the third footnote under the "Tax Ramifications" table in this chapter, if other sources had been used to make down payments for Houses #2 and #3, the equity could be $21,600 higher—the total balance remaining on the equity loans). This equity base of $222,237 can be viewed as a source of capital. Depending on the state of the financial markets and your own circumstances, you may want to tap this source for funding of future acquisitions.

Furthermore, this equity (after deductions for down payments on the house) represents additional earnings over the three years. To

Tax Ramifications

	Federal Income Taxes				State Income Taxes (Calif.)				Total Taxes Saved with Program		Tax Sheltered Income (Depreciation) with Program
Year End	Without Program	With Program	Savings	Percent	Without Program	With Program	Savings	Percent	Savings	Percent	
Pre-Program	$ 4,911	—	—	—	$ 938	—	—	—	—	—	—
Year 1	$ 5,047	$ 3,141	$ 1,906	37.8	$ 1,098	$ 589	$ 509	46.4	$ 2,415	39.3	$ 6,120
Year 2	$ 5,149	$ 1,990	$ 3,159	61.4	$ 1,289	$ 353	$ 936	72.6	$ 4,095	63.6	$ 11,220
Year 3	$ 5,550	$ 1,409	$ 4,141	74.6	$ 1,511	$ 229	$ 1,282	84.8	$ 5,423	76.8	$ 15,810
Totals (Years 1 through 3)	$ 15,746	$ 6,540	$ 9,206	58.4	$ 3,898	$ 1,171	$ 2,727	70.0	$ 11,933	60.7	$ 33,150

Property Values

	Total Value[a]				Equity[b]			
			Increase with Program				Increase with Program	
Year End	Without Program	With Program	Amount	Percent	Without Program	With Program	Amount	Percent
Pre-Program	$130,000	—	—	—	$ 78,000	—	—	—
Year 1	$149,500	$218,500	$ 69,000	46.2	$ 97,860	$119,100	$21,240	21.7
Year 2	$171,925	$320,275	$148,350	86.3	$120,645	$162,515[c]	$41,870	34.7
Year 3	$197,714	$437,317	$239,603	121.2	$146,794	$222,237[c,d]	$75,443	51.4
Totals	$197,714	$437,317	$239,603	121.2	$146,974	$222,237	$75,443	51.4

[a]Property in either case is assumed to increase by approximately 15% in each year. This reflects recent growth rates in the sunbelt areas such as Houston and Dallas.

[b]Assume only minor changes in mortgage balances: $360 per year on personal residence and $240 per year on each rental house.

[c]Calculation reflects a $12,000 equity loan on personal residence in addition to first mortgage obligation. Loan balance declines by $800 per year.

[d]Calculation reflects an equity loan of $12,000 on house #1, in addition to first mortgage obligation. Loan balance declines by $800 per year.

illustrate, by acquiring the three houses, and holding them, you have, as previously mentioned, $75,443 of additional equity. If you were to subtract the $36,000 of total down payments made on the three rental properties, the net amount, $39,443, has effectively been earned in the process. This translates into an additional $13,148 per year of earnings.

Recall that the gain for federal income tax purposes is only 40% taxable, if it qualifies for tax treatment as long-term capital gain (as in this case). To this amount we apply our marginal tax rate and thus obtain the tax owing. Since long-term capital gains are treated in this much more favorable light, they are to be sought after actively, as opposed to ordinary income (which is fully taxable). This program, then, as one can see, provides a mechanism for obtaining this favorable treatment. (For more detailed information on gain and taxation of gain, see Parts I and IV.)

You can now see that what started out as a tax-saving program has become quite an investment plan and a significant part of your overall tax estate and financial planning activity. By the way, if you were to continue this program, by the fourth or fifth house, depending on your own situation and itemized deductions, etc., you could be at the magic zero tax level. Congratulations would be in order!

The program detailed in the previous pages purposely used somewhat conservative figures for real estate appreciation, rental increases, and wage increases, relative to the experience in certain areas. In addition, the value and timing of the properties outlined was somewhat conservative. By doing this, I have attempted to build a program for the average taxpayer.

Certainly, if you purchase higher priced real property and do so at a faster rate than one a year, you could reduce your tax burden quicker and create a more substantial net worth in this shorter period. Likewise, if the appreciation of real property in the area is greater than the 15% noted in the guide, you only stand to benefit. If rents increase faster than noted or operating expenses are less than that projected, there will be less out-of-pocket expenses, but also lower tax write-off. If wages increase faster than noted, you will have a larger amount of gross income to offset but, correspondingly, you may be able to purchase more expensive properties due to your increased income level.

Every situation will be different and you will have to balance all the factors involved to determine the most beneficial route in terms of your personal and financial comfort.

As time passes, you will want to dispose of certain properties and buy/exchange others. This is done for a variety of reasons. For example, at a certain point in each property's life, depreciation and other deductions have decreased to the extent that another property would give greater tax benefit. Please be aware that when you reach the zero tax bracket ($3,400 of taxable income or less for a married couple filing jointly), if you sell a property for a long-term capital gain, there may still be a tax on the gain. This is due to the alternative minimum tax section in the Code. This will be discussed further in Part IV, along with sales and other dispositions of real property.

Part IV

Disposition of Real Property

20

Introduction

Sooner or later a disposition of one or more of your income properties may be desired or necessary for one reason or another. Two common situations necessitating disposition are the need for cash (with no other suitable sources at the time) and the need for additional tax shelter.

The term *disposition* can be defined in many ways. However, in the context of this Part, it will include the following:

1. Outright sale
2. Sale of remainder interest
3. Sale of one-half interest
4. Option sale
5. Escrow sale
6. Installment sale
7. Private annuity and reverse annuity mortgage
8. Devise
9. Gift
10. Pyramiding through refinancing
11. Tax-free exchange
12. Land lease
13. Joint tenancy

Of course, several of the aforementioned devices might be used in conjunction with another as will be described in later chapters. However, you should be aware of and understand all of the devices. In this manner, you can select the proper method of disposition to meet your needs and financial circumstances.

21

Outright Sale

You have a property that you have held more than one year, wish to sell it, and have the transaction completed—leaving you in a cashed-out position. You can then utilize the funds received (after taxes) for other purposes. You no longer have any economic interest in the property. This situation outlines an outright sale.

What are the tax ramifications of this outright sale? If there is a gain recognized and you have held this property for investment purposes or as a trade or business, the gain will be treated as long-term capital gain for income tax purposes. If there is a loss recognized, the designation of the property becomes critically important. Generally speaking, if the property was held for investment purposes, the loss is treated as a long-term capital loss, in which case you will only be able to deduct one-half of these long-term capital losses against ordinary income up to a maximum of $3,000. If the net capital loss exceeds $1,000, the balance can be carried forward to the next year as an offset to capital gains with one-half of the excess deductible against ordinary income to a maximum of again $3,000. The carryforward benefits continue until the net capital loss is exhausted or until your death.

However, if you have operated these properties as a trade or business and there has been a loss recognized, it is treated as an *ordinary* loss. This means that it can be used directly, dollar for dollar, to offset ordinary income, with the only limitation being the amount of your own ordinary income. Thus, you can readily see that it is better, in a net capital loss situation (if any loss situation is ever good), to be using these properties as a trade or business.

How do you calculate the gain (or loss)? The gain (or loss) realized in a sale is the difference between the amount realized on the sale and your adjusted basis in the property sold. (Realized gain will equal recognized gain as a general rule, unless another Code section provides otherwise—for example, see "Tax-free Exchange," Chapter 27.) The amount realized is the sales price less brokers' commissions and other sales expenses. Note that the amount realized *includes* the indebtedness on that property (the mortgage balance).

Adjusted basis is determined in the following manner:

It is the (1) basis in the property (in this case normally the original cost of the property),

plus (2) broker's commissions, attorneys' fees, appraisal costs, escrow charges, and other acquisition costs,

plus (3) capital improvements,

plus (4) taxes, interest, insurance, and other charges that the taxpayer has elected to *capitalize*,

minus (5) depreciation, obsolescence, amortization, and depletion deductions allowed, but not less than the amount allowable.

For example, assume it is January 2, four years after you began your program, and you wish to sell House #3 for $69,000 (It was purchased January 1 of Year 3). Thus, the gain, if any, would be characterized as long-term capital gain, with the exception of the gain attributable to the excess depreciation deductions (attributable to use of the accelerated depreciation method). This latter amount is recaptured as ordinary income.

The house originally cost $60,000 and, associated with the acquisition, assume that there were $1,500 in acquisition costs. You claimed $6,120 in depreciation in Year 3. Selling expenses (commissions: $3,600; other selling costs: $1,800) total $5,400. The *amount realized* on the sale is calculated as follows:

Sales Price		$ 69,000
Less: Commissions	$3,600	
Other sales expense	1,800	(5,400)
Amount realized		$ 63,600
Adjusted basis is calculated as below:		
Original (cost) basis:		$ 60,000
Plus: acquisition costs		1,500
		$ 61,500
Less: Depreciation		(6,120)
Adjusted basis		$ 55,380
Gain realized on the sale is:		
Amount realized		$ 63,600
Less: Adjusted basis		(55,380)
Gain realized (and recognized)		$ 8,220

Long-term capital gains receive very favorable tax treatment. It is a fact that 60% of the gain is excluded from federal income taxes. However, before this exclusion is calculated, the amount of the gain attributed to excess depreciation deductions must be subtracted from the gain realized above. Since excess depreciation amounted to $2,720 in this case ($6,120 less the straight-line amount of $3,400), the long-term capital gain totals $5,500. Of this amount, $3,300 is yours *tax-free*. The remaining 40%, or $2,200, is taxable at your marginal tax rate, as is the $2,720 that is recaptured as ordinary income. The maximum federal income tax rate on ordinary income is 50%. Thus, the highest composite federal income tax on the total capital gain is 20% (40% times 50%).

Note, however, that state income tax treatment of capital gains may differ. For example, in California, if the property were held between one and five years, only 35% would be excluded; however, if it were held more than five years, 50% would be excluded from California income tax. The maximum rate at which the included amount can be taxed (in California) is 11%.

What is the tax on the above transaction? Assuming you have reduced your federal taxable income to $13,923 (owing a tax of $1,409 on this amount), the additional tax as a result of the sale of House #3 could approximate $791. The California tax would approach $291. Thus, total taxes due to the sale are $1,082, leaving a net *after-tax* gain of $7,138. If instead you had received an additional $8,220 in wages, your federal and California income taxes would have been approximately $1,448 and $406, respectively, for a total of $1,854. You would have lost almost 23% of these additional wages.

You can easily conclude that obtaining capital gains is a much more satisfactory and productive method of making money, even if some of the depreciation is recaptured as ordinary income. *(Note*: All figures assume a married couple filing jointly, both under 65 years old, with two minor children living at home in California.)

You must be aware, however, that an *alternative minimum tax* section exists in the Internal Revenue Code, should you lower your taxable income to below the "zero bracket amount" and have a long-term capital gain. The calculation of alternative minimum taxable income is far too complex for this type of discussion. Suffice it to say that because the section exists does not necessarily mean that there will be an alternative minimum tax imposed. If the calculation of alternative minimum taxable income, which includes among other things gross income reduced by deductions, plus the 60% of the gain normally excluded less the deductions (except for your personal residence), plus the amount of *itemized* deductions such as interest and charitable contributions which exceeds 60% of your *adjusted* gross income reduced by medical expense, tax (state/local/foreign), casualty losses, and some estate taxes, is less than or equal to $20,000, there is no alternative minimum tax. For the next $40,000, there is a 10% tax; and on any amounts in excess of $60,000 (total), there is a 20% tax. In this case, there would be no alternative minimum tax. As with all of this program, a competent tax attorney or CPA can detail this alternative minimum tax provision.

Generally, unless there is some extraordinary reason, it may not be the wisest thing to dispose of income properties in this manner. There are more beneficial methods to raise capital, such as equity loans and refinancing, where the loan proceeds come to you *tax-free* and interest is deductible. There are better ways to dispose of current properties and obtain others—such as tax-free exchanges— to improve tax shelter, to save taxes, or for other reasons. All of these will be discussed later in this Part. If you feel that you must sell one of your properties at least consider selling it, if you can, on an installment basis or by use of another sales device as described in the following chapters.

If the property to be sold is your personal residence, you should review the Overview for discussion of special rules in this regard.

22

Sales of Remainder Interest and One-Half Interest

Remainder Interest

There is a method whereby you can sell your property, use the property during your lifetime, and save estate taxes in the process. It sounds inconsistent, doesn't it? How can you use your property and sell it to others at the same time? Let me explain. Ownership of real property is actually an ownership of interests—a life estate and a remainder. A life estate allows the owner to use and enjoy the property during his lifetime. The remainder interest is a part which allows the use and enjoyment of the property after the life tenant's death.

An owner of real property can very wisely use this device to benefit his children. For example, a parent sells the *remainder* interest in the real property to his children; the parent lives on or uses the property until he dies, and then the remaindermen (the children) have use of the property. Since the life estate owned by the parent terminates at his death, the real property is completely removed from his estate, thus saving estate taxes.

There are a few items of which to be aware in this type of sale. First, the sale of the remainder interest must be for full and adequate consideration. It *cannot* be a gift or the property will be subject to estate taxes at the parents' death. Second, monies or promissory notes received by the parents *will* be subject to estate taxes, if they are still in the parent's estate at the time of his death.

Of course, the parent could give these monies or promissory notes away tax-free (using the $10,000 annual tax-free gift exclusion discussed earlier) and, thus, remove them from his estate. Furthermore, if the parent does die with these monies or promissory notes still in his estate, the amount paid by his children for their remainder interest will be significantly less than the market value of this interest if it had been included in full in the parents' estate at the time of death, assuming continued appreciation of real estate. Third, it must be noted that this sale may generate taxable capital gain to the parent. Fourth, due to certain provisions in the Code, certain depreciation and other deductions could be lost to the parent. (You should consult your attorney for advice.)

One-Half Interest

Let's assume you own a property that you believe is going to appreciate significantly over time. However, your mortgage payments are so large that you cannot continue to make the payments much longer. Somehow, you would like to keep the property. At this point your concern is not primarily with saving taxes, but first and foremost holding on to the property and generating a return.

The solution is to sell a one-half interest in the property for some nominal figure (e. g., $1.00, $10.00). The purchaser of this one-half interest would assume the existing loan, thus obligating himself to make the monthly mortgage payments. You have kept an interest in the property and yet have relieved yourself of the burdensome loan payments. The purchaser has obtained an interest in a good growth property with a miniscule down payment. (*Note:* The loan would have to be assumable or the financial institution would have to consent to this transaction.)

Upon the later sale of the property, the proceeds would be equally divided. The purchaser would pay off the existing loan balance from his share of the proceeds. Assuming a one year holding period, these profits would be treated as capital gains.

23

Option, Escrow, and Installment Sales

Option Sales

An option (contract) in terms of real estate is a right to buy or sell property. With a true option contract, only one of the parties is bound and the other party is free to exercise or forfeit the right to buy at his option. It differs from a sales contract in that a sales contract binds both parties to the contract—one to buy and the other to sell. Note that an option contract that calls for a disproportionately large option price will probably be treated as a sales contract. Similarly, if the so-called option contract calls for immediate transfer of possession and the payment of the full price over an agreed period in installments, it will be treated as a sales contract. As a special note, the terms of the option should be specific as to the disposition of the option payment if the option is not exercised. This avoids taxation of this payment in the year of receipt.

Why did I mention these options? There are three primary considerations: *cash flow, timing of the sale, and taxes.*

Cash Flow

An option contract granting the potential purchaser an option to purchase the property at an agreed price to be paid in the future allows you, the seller, to receive a part of the total consideration for the property in a year prior to the year of sale with no tax due on the payement. No tax is owing until the year in which the option is exercised or forfeited by the purchaser.

Timing of Sale

An option contract could be used to effectively postpone the date of sale until after the one year holding period has elapsed, so as to qualify for capital gains treatment. Again, be careful that the option is a true option (described above). Otherwise, the option payment could be viewed as the equivalent of a down payment on a completed sale *prior* to the expiration of the one year holding period and, thus, any gain on the sale would be treated as ordinary income.

An option contract could also allow an otherwise very good buyer willing to pay an attractive price, but who temporarily does not have the funds, to purchase the property. If he can show that he can raise the funds later, you could utilize the timing aspect of an option for your benefit. Also, an option might be used in times of tight money or where funds are simply not available. When they are available, the option can be exercised by the purchaser. And, all the while, you would have had control of the property's appreciation for a relatively modest amount.

Tax Ramifications

There are significant tax ramifications. As previously mentioned, you can receive the option payment in one year without incurring any tax until the transaction is closed. If the option is exercised by the purchaser, the portion paid previously for the option (consideration) is treated as part of the total purchase price of the property. If the property has been held more than one year, the gain, if any, qualifies for long-term capital gains treatment.

If the holder of the option (the optionee) does not exercise the option and you retain the consideration paid, it is taxable to you as ordinary income in the year the option expired. (To the optionee, it is a loss and tax treatment depends on the holding period.) However, if you return the consideration paid for the option to the optionee, there is no tax to you despite the fact that you have had the use of the consideration for the option period. The return to the optionee is also a non-taxable event to him. (It is treated as a return of funds.)

An example may help to illustrate these tax consequences. Assume that you grant the buyer an option to purchase one of your rental houses, which you have held for nine months, for a price of $100,000 anytime after three months but within the next twelve months. The option payment paid to you amounts to $5,000. Assume for this example only that the adjusted basis of the property is $60,000 and there are no brokers' commissions or other sales expenses. Also assume only straight-line depreciation has been used.

TAX CONSEQUENCES

Event		Gain
When taxpayer-seller grants the option:		—
When the optionee fails to exercise the option:		$5,000 ordinary income
When the optionee exercises the option:		
Sales price	$100,000	
Plus: Option consideration	5,000	
Subtotal	$105,000	
Less: Adjusted basis	(60,000)	$45,000 long-term capital gain (only 40% or $18,000 taxable at your marginal rate)
If the taxpayer-seller had sold the property after holding it for 9 months (without granting any option):		
Sales price	$100,000	
Less: Adjusted basis	(60,000)	$40,000 of *ordinary* income (all taxable at your marginal rate)

You can see that you have the use of $5,000 *tax-free* until the option is exercised or fails. If the optionee fails to exercise the option, you have $5,000 in ordinary income *in the year of expiration*, after having used these funds without reduction for tax. Finally, when the optionee exercises the option, the holding period for the property has exceeded one year, making the gain of $45,000 eligible for favorable capital gains treatment. An outright sale at the time you could have granted the option results in $40,000 of ordinary income. The difference in taxable gain in the latter two cases is $22,000. For a married couple (both under 65 years old) filing jointly with two minor children (without reference to any other deductions) and assuming no other income besides either the aforementioned capital gain or the ordinary income, the difference in federal income tax could amount to several thousand dollars if the option contract is not used. In addition, without an option contract, you have in actual dollars received, $5,000 less.

Of course, the use of an option contract in a period of high inflation must be done with caution. That is, the sales price should reflect the anticipated inflationary effect over the option period.

The "lease-option" is just an application of the option contract. For example, a lessee would normally pay $400 of rent per month. With a lease option granted by the lessor-owner, the rent could approach $550 to $600. The $150 to $200 increase represents the amount by which the lessee-buyer values the option. This amount is the option payment and, if the lessee exercises the option within the prescribed time period, these option payments are credited to the purchase price. All of the aforementioned option contract discussion and rules apply.

Escrow Sales

Since the date of the closing of the sales escrow is generally accepted as the date of sale, a wise use of the escrow will enable you, the taxpayer-seller, to control the tax year in which the sales proceeds are reportable for tax purposes. For example, keeping the escrow open until the running of the one-year holding period for long-term capital gains, you can derive the considerable tax benefit from this type of gain instead of suffering with ordinary gain. If escrow closes in the tax year following the year in which the contract of sale was actually executed, you can, in effect, transfer gain to a year in which your income may be less.

To properly *use* the escrow process, you *must not abuse* it. Therefore, if all performances on both sides are complete and the escrow holder merely waits until the new year to roll around and then pays you your funds and delivers the deed to the buyer, this will not work. For tax purposes, you will be deemed to have received the funds in the prior tax year. To avoid this result, you and the purchaser should not complete all performances until after the new year begins. This way the contract is merely executory.

Another common pitfall is to grant possession to the purchaser, believing that retention of legal title will keep escrow open. Again the sale is treated as being completed in the previous tax year.

The point is that intelligent use of the escrow process in conjunction with other types of disposition can have significant beneficial impact for you. A competent escrow officer, real estate agent, or other professional should be utilized.

Installment Sales

An installment sale is a sale where at least one payment is to be received after the close of the taxable year in which the disposition occurs. You, the seller, will usually take back a promissory note on the unpaid balance. The motivation for such a sale arises primarily from the net results of that sale:

1. Since the gain can be received over a period of years, the possibility of reduced taxes exists.
2. Since the payment of the total contract price can be spread over several years, the buyer may be able to more easily afford (and you more easily sell) the property.

The installment sale method is not a complicated technique, and recent changes in the law ("Installment Sales Revision Act of 1980") have, in effect, operated to relax many of the former technical requirements, as well as more clearly define the situations under which the method is available. (You should consult a tax attorney or other qualified professional to determine if/ensure that your sale qualifies.) And, note that the installment sale method applies to gain only, not to losses.

I will highlight some of the changes affecting the subject matter of this guide and contrast them to the old rules:

Selling Price

With the new Act, the former requirement that the seller not receive in excess of 30% of the purchase price as the initial payment in the year of sale is eliminated. Instead, under the new Act, the initial payment can be *any* or *no* amount at all.

Also, with the new Act, the former requirement of a fixed, firm selling price is eliminated. Under the new Act, installment sale treatment is available for sales involving a contingent sales price (and even an indefinite payment period).

Number of payments

With the new Act, the old requirement that the sale involve two or more payments of the purchase price in two or more taxable years is eliminated. Under the new Act, the number of payments is irrelevant. In fact, *no* installments are required. For example, if a sale called for a single payment to be made after the close of the year of sale, it would qualify for installment sale treatment.

Election

With the new Act, the requirement of electing installment sale treatment is eliminated. Instead, under the new Act, this treatment is *automatic*, unless the taxpayer elects (on or before the filing date of the income tax return in the year in which the sale occurs) not to have this treatment apply.

Unstated interest

If the contract does not indicate a specific rate of interest or one that is less than 9% (simple) per year, interest is imputed by the Government at 10% compounded semi-annually. (The only exception involves the sale of land between family members, spouses, siblings, ancestors, and lineal decendents. In that case, a maximum 7% rate is imputed on sales where the aggregate sales price of such land totals less than $500,000.) This, in turn, effectively reduces the selling price (by the amount of imputed interest). The result is that the initial payment would often exceed the old 30% requirement. Under the new Act, this problem is eliminated as the 30% requirement, as previously mentioned, is abolished. However, you generally should still specify an interest rate of 9% or above, because imputed interest can create other difficulties, which include the fact that this imputed interest can change what otherwise would have qualified as capital gain into ordinary income. (Note that if the sale price were $3,000 or less, or if there are no payments due more than one year from the date of the disposition, unstated interest is not imputed and the aforementioned discussion can be disregarded.)

Sales of depreciable property to related persons

Under the old law, installment sale treatment was available for sales of depreciable property to family members. With the new Act, this type of sale is not barred, but it is subject to rather strict rules. That is, under the new Act, any time a taxpayer sells depreciable property to his spouse or certain (see later discussion, Chapter 30 on sales to "related persons") 80% owned partnerships or corporations, the deferred payments are deemed to have been received in the taxable year in which the sale occurs. Thus, in these situations, the installment method of treating the gain is not available. (Note that if the taxpayer can show that no tax motive is involved, then the treatment may apply. A basic example would involve two taxpayers, formerly husband and wife, but now divorced. If he sold the depreciable property to her, this sale would most likely qualify for installment sale treatment.)

Retroactivity

Under the new Act, two former provisions (the "30% rule" and the "two payment rule") are dropped retroactively. What this means is that a sale made on or before October 19, 1980, which didn't qualify because it didn't meet either or both of these two aforementioned requirements, can now qualify for installment sale treatment. However, it qualifies under the law applicable *as of the date of the sale*, with the exception of the two aforementioned rules.

The computation of installment gain is fairly straightforward, but allow me to detail the definition in legalese. The installment gain is that gain recognized in any taxable year equal to that proportion of the installment payment received in that year which the "gross profit realized" (or to be realized when payment is completed) bears to the "total contract price." In this case, *gross profit realized* is that amount realized after deducting sales expenses. The *total contract price* is that amount received or to be received by the seller, excluding any existing mortgage assumed, except to the extent to which it exceeds the seller's basis.

The best way to understand this concept of installment gain is to undertake an example. Going back to the sale of our House #3 as discussed in Chapter 21, the sales price was $69,000. After deducting sales expenses of $5,400, the amount realized was $63,600. Deducted from this amount was the adjusted basis of $55,380, leaving a gain realized, or, in this case, "gross profit realized," of $8,220. Assume you sell the property on the installment method and will receive four equal payments over four years. Your installment gain is thus:

$$\text{Installment Gain} = \text{"payment received"} \times \frac{\text{"gross profit realized"}}{\text{"total contract price"}}$$

$$= \$17,250 \qquad\qquad \times \frac{\$ 8,220}{\$69,000}$$

$$= \underline{\underline{\$ 2,055}}$$

In this case, since you are receiving four equal installments, the installment gain in each year will be the same.

The installment gain is taxed in the same manner as previously described in Chapter 21. The house was held for at least one year and, thus, gain realized (and recognized) is eligible, to the extent not attributable to excess depreciation, for long-term capital gains treatment. In this instance, the excess depreciation totaled $2,720 of the total $8,220 gain or 33.1%. Thus, 66.9% or $1,375 of the installment gain ($2,055) is characterized as long-term capital gain. Only 40% of this amount or $550 is taxable. To this, add the portion of the installment gain which results from use of the accelerated depreciation method. The sum of these two figures is taxable at your marginal rate:

Federal Income Tax
on Installment Gain = (40% of capital gain + excess depreciation) × marginal tax rate
= ($550 + $680) × 16%[a]
= $186[b]

---

[a] Assumes 16% marginal rate attained with a federal taxable income of $13,923 (before accounting for the installment gain).
[b] Includes the effects of state income tax on the federal tax calculation. (See discussion below.) Ignoring these effects, the federal tax would equal $197: ($550 + $680) × 16%.

If you were to remain in that same 16% tax bracket over the four years, or if your other income decreases or you have additional deductions that place you in a lower tax bracket in the last three years of the installment sale period, then a sale under the installment sale method will save you tax dollars over an outright sale. This is due to the fact that, in an outright sale, the entire taxable part of the gain ($4,920) would be added to your other ordinary income in one year. This will push you into the next marginal tax bracket, thus resulting in more tax. (*Note:* The calculation of California income tax would be similar to that undertaken for the federal income tax, except that 65% of the capital gain would be taxable, and a 4% marginal rate is used, with a resulting tax of $63.) Of course, the interest earned on any promissory note is ordinary income and is taxable as ordinary income.

In an installment sale, there is an additional factor to be considered. The longer the payment period, the less the value these future payments have in terms of today's dollars. In a period of high inflation, then, these future payments might be discounted substantially and, therefore, may make this type of sale less attractive. Of course, the importance of this factor is tempered by the other considerations involved: the circumstances of the sale, your tax status, the discount rate, and the duration of the installment period.

24

Private Annuity and Reverse Annuity Mortgage

Private Annuity

You are worried that you will live so long that your estate will be exhausted before you die. You are reaching a point in life where you only want to receive income on your investments without any hassles associated with the production of this income. And, if possible, you would like to help your children *and* save on estate taxes. Is this possible? Yes, through the use of a private annuity.

An annuity (in general) works like this: The person who sets up the annuity (the beneficiary) transfers property worth a certain current market value. In return, he is to receive monthly income payments for life. The monthly payments are made by the transferee (the purchaser of the property). The amount of the payments is based upon the fair market value of the property at the time of the transfer, the age and life expectancy of the beneficiary, and current interest rates. The annuity amount is determined through the use of actuarial tables similar to those used by life insurance people. The payments are to continue until the beneficiary's death, upon which time they immediately cease.

Advantages

This device could be used effectively between parent and child. The parent would be the beneficiary of the annuity and would transfer property to the child in return for monthly income annuity payments for the remainder of the parent's life. Thus, the property transferred and future appreciation, as well as the annuity, would be excluded from the parent's taxable estate. The child benefits economically in cases where the life expectancy is not great. Thus, the child's annuity payments on such a property could be much less than the actual current value of the property.

Disadvantages

As with any device, there are disadvantages and other considerations. The private annuity is no exception. First, since life expectancy is often shorter than an installment period in an installment sale, the transferees often pay significantly higher monthly payments in a private annuity than under an installment sale. This could present some cash flow problems, especially for a child just building his income stream. However, this problem could be offset somewhat by the parent making annual tax-free gifts in forgiving part of the annuity payment.

Second, the promise to pay the monthly income payments to the beneficiary is *unsecured*. This is in contrast to the installment sale, where the installment note is secured by a deed of trust on the property. Because of this lack of security, a good, trusting relationship must exist between beneficiary and transferee. This is why these private annuities are made generally between parent and child.

Third, part of each payment made by the child is interest and is reportable by the transferor (parent) as interest income. However, the transferee (child) *cannot* deduct this from his gross income, as in the case of interest paid on an installment note under an installment sale.

Fourth, the transfer of this property is treated as a sale of the property. Thus, it is subject to income tax. Part of each annuity payments is treated as gain from the sale of the property. If the property has been held for a year or more, the gain is treated as long-term capital gain, ameliorating part of the income tax effects.

Fifth, the transferee's (child's) cost basis is not determined until the death of the transferor (parent). It is only at that time that the total consideration paid by the child can be determined. The child's cost basis will be the sum of the annuity payments made during the parent's life. If the parent is in poor health and dies soon after the annuity arrangement is created, the child will have a very low cost basis in the property. Thus, upon resale of the property later by the child, his gain will be much larger than if he had purchased the property from the parent in an outright or installment sale. In these latter types of sales, the child's basis would be the current market value of the property when transferred (with adjustments as discussed in Chapter 2).

Sixth, if the transferor (parent) lives beyond his life expectancy, the transferee (child) could wind up paying more for the property than if he had purchased it outright from the parent, since the monthly annuity payments are based partly on the life expectancy of the parent (transferor).

Further, the value of the property to be transferred must be established prior to the transfer. This may require an independent appraisal—at additional cost.

Reverse Annuity Mortgage

The reverse annuity mortgage (RAM) is very closely allied to the general annuity concept. At the same time, it is a mortgage. However, it is unlike most mortgages with which you may be familiar. In this case, the lender pays *you* monthly payments. He does this because you have built up equity in your property against which you have taken out a loan. As the lender makes payments to you, your loan balance gradually increases to a predetermined maximum amount. Most RAM's are due in 10 years. At that time, you would either refinance the house or sell.

Another type of RAM exists—the "fixed debt with life annuity RAM." In this instance, an interest-only loan is made to the borrower and the loan amount is then used to purchase an annuity from a life insurance company. From the annuity, the life insurance company makes the loan payments, with the balance paid to the borrower. The mortgage is due in 10 years or upon the sale of property, whichever occurs first.

The major attraction for these RAM devices is the fact that an annuity can be obtained utilizing the previously idle equity in the property and no out-of-pocket expense is incurred. However, the underlying real property is still in the borrower's net estate, even if a part of the equity may not be anymore.

Actually, the tax and financial considerations regarding the RAM are unclear at this time since it is a new concept and not well understood. Some of the financial institutions are presently confused by it and, consequently, it is not being widely offered.

25

Devise and Gift

Devise

Devise is the term used for a gift of real property by will. If there is someone to whom you would like to leave a property after you die, you could dispose of this property by will and both you and your estate could avoid *ever* paying any income tax on the disposition. In addition, the beneficiary obtains the property without paying any income taxes on the transaction.

The beneficiary obtains the property with a "stepped-up" basis equal to the fair market value on date of death or, for federal income tax purposes, on the alternate valuation date, if elected by the representative of the estate. (That alternative date is now six months from the date of the death.) The fact that the basis is stepped-up is very significant, since calculation of taxable gain makes use of the basis amount. If you recall, the gain realized is the difference between amount realized and *adjusted basis*. Thus, the higher the adjusted basis, the less the gain, and the lower the taxes.

An example will assist in outlining the true income tax benefits involved. Assume that the owner of a rental house wishes to leave his son this property (and indicates so in his will). The owner purchased the house for $60,000 (with $1,500 of acquisition costs) and upon his death it has a fair market value of $100,000. The owner had taken $19,890 in depreciation deductions. (Assume for simplicity that the deceased's estate repays the mortgage.) After a probate period, the son receives the title to the property. The deceased owner (or his estate) has paid no income tax on this transfer, even though there is a "gain" on the property of $58,390: $100,000 sales price less the $41,610 adjusted basis ($60,000 cost plus $1,500 acquisition costs, less $19,890 in depreciation expense). In effect, the son has realized this gain since the property has been transferred to him. Yet, the gain is not recognized. Inheritances are not generally the equivalent of income for income tax purposes. Thus, the son does not pay any income tax, despite the fact that he just received an asset valued at $100,000. To compare: If you earned an additional $100,000 in wages, up to 50% could be taxable, depending on your individual circumstances.

To further illustrate, assume a year later the property is worth $115,000. Holding title to the property, the son decides he wants to sell. His sales expenses are $10,350. The son had also operated the property as a "trade or business" (renting it out) and assume his depreciation deduction, using the accelerated method, was $10,200. What are the federal income tax consequences?

Calculation of Gain with "Stepped-up" Basis

Sales Price		$115,000
Less: Commission	$6,900	
Other sales expenses	3,450	(10,350)
Amount realized		$104,650
Adjusted basis is calculated as below:		
Original basis		$100,000
Less: Depreciation		(10,200)
Adjusted basis		$ 89,800
Gain realized on the sale:		
Amount realized		$104,650
Less: Adjusted basis		(89,800)
Gain realized (and recognized)		$ 14,850

Assuming the son, prior to this sale, would have had a $20,000 taxable income (and he filed jointly with his wife), the federal tax on the aforementioned transaction would approximate $2,019, excluding any state tax effects. If the son had received the property from his father and his father's adjusted basis the gain and resulting tax would have been markedly higher. The gain in that case would be:

Calculation of Gain Without "Stepped-up" Basis

Original (cost) basis	$60,000
Plus: Acquisition costs	1,500
	61,500
Less: Depreciation	(19,890)
Father's adjusted basis at death	41,610
The son's adjusted basis is thus:	
Son's original basis	$41,610
Less: Depreciation	(10,200)
Son's adjusted basis	$31,410
The gain realized by the son would now be:	
Amount realized	$104,650
Less: Adjusted basis	(31,410)
Gain realized (and recognized)	$ 73,240

With the above gain, the tax soars to $9,673 or almost *five* times that previously. Obviously, if the son were in a higher bracket, the tax would be overwhelming.

Additionally, if the son is in a low income tax bracket (or none at all), the income that he does receive from the rents (if he operates this house as a "trade or business" and has a positive cash flow) could be taxed significantly less than if the father had received this income (if the father had been in a high bracket).

The fact that there are no income taxes owing on the disposition of a property by means of a will does not mean necessarily that the transaction is entirely free of tax consequences. Taxes that may be owing are estate and inheritance taxes. Estate tax is imposed on the *right to transfer* property, and is imposed on the decedent's net estate as a whole, which includes property owned at death (as above) and certain property transferred by the decedent during his lifetime. Explanation of the method used to determine the value of the net estate will be left to a future work by this author or your tax attorney. What you should keep in mind, however, is that not all estates have estate taxes imposed on them. The Ecomomic Recovery Act of 1981 provides for a phase-in of unified credits against estate and gift taxes. The net result is that, for decedents dying in the next few years, increasingly larger estates will escape federal estate taxes as seen below.

Year of Death	Amount that Gross Estate Would Have to Exceed Before Estate Tax is Due ("Equivalent Exemption")
1982	$225,000
1983	275,000
1984	325,000
1985	400,000
1986	500,000
1987 and later	600,000

Note that each person has the aforementioned equivalent exemptions. (There may or may not be some form of state estate tax applicable.)

An inheritance tax, on the other hand, is imposed by a majority of states on the *right to receive* property, and the tax liability is based on each beneficiary's distributive share. Each beneficiary is liable for the tax on his share, although the tax may be payable by the administrator or executor of the estate. In addition, beneficiaries are classified based on degree of relationship with the decedent, with lower tax rates and higher exemptions from taxes available to those beneficiaries of closer degree. If the tax is paid by the executor/ administrator or the amount of property transferred is exempt, the beneficiary has received the property totally free of inheritance tax.

Note that if the property is community property and the deceased leaves his one-half share to the other spouse, the aforementioned paragraphs apply. Both halves of the community property receive a step-up in basis but only *one-half* (the decedent's interest) is included in his gross estate.

You have to assess your own situation, but disposition by will may be one of the best methods to avoid income tax and yet benefit a loved one greatly, by providing financial security to a degree, largely free of taxes. However, this type of disposition must be coordinated with your overall estate plan, which may include trusts and other estate planning devices. Note that individual state law will differ in this area and should be carefully investigated.

Gift

A gifting program is generally a key part of any estate plan. The advantages generally outweigh the disadvantages. The advantages include potentially reducing income and estate taxes; helping a child/relative/friend to enjoy a higher standard of living; shielding the family unit against future possible creditor problems (although gifts cannot be made in fraud of creditors—such as in the case of a gift made after incurring a liability); removing assets from probate; and eliminating management problems for the donor. The disadvantages include potential misuse of the gift by the donee; elimination of a degree of security in the event of a financial setback; the passing of the gift to those whom the donor had no intention of benefitting (a result of the donee predeceasing the donor); and potential family disharmony.

Gifts can be outright gifts, as is often the case, or gifts in trust. The latter type of gift could be undertaken for a number of reasons. For example, the donee might be too young to manage the asset or he might be a spendthrift, incapable of effectively handling monetary affairs. The tax aspects of gifts in trust vary widely, depending on the type of trust involved. A discussion on that subject would go beyond the scope of this guide and, therefore, is not included here.

Proper selection of the beneficiary of your kindness can be crucial. Of course, if taxes are of no concern, then you would make a gift of any amount to anyone you choose. However, if taxes do matter, then the following considerations should enter into the donor's choice of donees.

Taxes

With regard to *gift taxes,* a donor can make an unlimited gift to his spouse without incurring gift taxes. A gift to anyone else, generally speaking, can only total a maximum of $10,000 per year without incurring gift tax. Of course, you and your wife can jointly give a total of $20,000 without gift tax consequences.

With regard to *estate taxes,* if reduction of estate taxes is the goal of your gifting program, then interspousal gifts are good but not as good as gifts to your children. Gifts between spouses only reduce estate taxes upon the death of the first spouse (unless the survivor eliminates these amounts from her estate). However, gifts made to children reduce estate taxes on the death of each spouse.

As to *income taxes,* a gift of an income-producing asset to a child will generally save more income taxes than a gift to a spouse. This is due to the child's low tax bracket as opposed to a spouses's high bracket—maybe the maximum 50% marginal rate.

Methods

Assuming you feel that the advantages outweigh the disadvantages, a gift of your real property may be in order. Remember that a couple can jointly make annual gifts of $20,000 to any number of persons without incurring federal gift tax. At the same time, you want to get the property out of your estate (as well as the future appreciation in value). Finally, since the property is income producing, you want to shift the income to those with lower tax brackets (that is, if the income has not been sheltered).

You can do this in one of two ways utilizing gifts. Assume you and your spouse own real property worth $60,000 and you have three children. You and your spouse together could give the real property to your children as tenants in common, with each having a one-third (or $20,000 interest initially) in the property. Thus, each has received a $20,000 gift. Or you could (if you are able) give each of the children $20,000 in cash and they could purchase the property from you. However, you cannot condition the "gift" upon a certain performance by the children. This would not qualify as a valid gift.

Either method reduces your estate by eliminating the real property value and its future appreciation. Furthermore, in either case, the income produced by the real property would be earned by others, thus reducing your income taxes (of course, hopefully, the tax shelter in the real property should have minimized the taxable income).

However, the choice of method makes a difference in several areas. First, if the children are given cash and then they purchase the house from you, their basis in the property would be their cost—$60,000—and not your old low basis if you had given the real property to them. Thus, they would prefer the cash gifts. On the other hand, the parents would prefer a gift of the real property itself since there is no income to be reported in this gift transaction. However, if the parents gave the children cash, and the children purchased the real property from the parents, the parents would have a taxable capital gain or, worse yet, ordinary income (if the property was not held for at least one year). Thus, all considerations of a gift must be taken into account before proceeding.

26

Pyramiding Through Refinancing

Actually, using this concept, you, the taxpayer, will *keep* all of your properties. The basic idea is that you will be attempting to improve your rate of return on the presently owned property, and to obtain as much of the value of the property as possible in loan form so that you can use these funds to purchase additional properties. By purchasing more properties, you are increasing your tax shelter.

You are, in effect, using the property as a bank. If you refinance a house, you are obtaining a new loan of an amount greater than the old loan, and the old loan is retired. For example, you may have a property with a loan balance of $45,000 but the fair market value of that property is $100,000. Knowing that financial institutions will generally loan up to approximately 80% of the value of the property, you obtain a new $80,000 loan on the property and pay off the $45,000 balance on the old loan.

Most mortgage loan documents include a prepayment (penalty) clause. That is, if you prepay more than a specified percentage (for example 20%) of the loan principal balance in any 12 months or the specified period, as you would if you refinanced the property, you will be subjected to a penalty. The amount of that penalty can be severe—often 6 months' interest. Note that the clause may be written so as to have effect throughout the term of the loan, although some loan documents indicate a specified period in which the penalty will be exacted—the first five years of the loan is common. However, if you refinance through the same financial institution that made the original loan, often it will not enforce the prepayment (penalty) clause, since in many cases the interest rate on the new loan is higher than the old and, thus, it helps the institution's portfolio yield.

The net result of the aforementioned transaction is that you received $35,000 ($80,000 − $45,000) to use to buy additional properties. You might be able to place down payments on several houses with this amount depending on the price of the houses, your ability to support the payments, and whether the properties are self-supporting. These loan proceeds come to you *tax-free*. In addition, you have the additional interest deduction these loans create. Furthermore, the rate of return is improved because less cash is sitting idle in the current property.

The timing of this refinancing technique can be critical. Of course, the properties to refinance are those that have had the greatest appreciation, and the refinancing should be attempted when interest rates are lower than otherwise. This necessitates watching the financing markets and trends. However, even in times of high interest rates, refinancing should still be considered.

High interest rates, per se, should not frighten you away from solid real estate investment. Actually, these rates are a bargain if you look at the net cost of interest after taxes. For example, if the interest rate is 15% and you are in a 33% marginal tax bracket, your after-tax cost is only 10%. If inflation is 10% annually, the net cost of this interest is *zero*—you have had the use of this money free of charge. Compare this situation to the experience in the early 1960's. With mortgage interest rates then at a now unheard of low of 6%, a 33% tax bracket individual had an after-tax cost of 4%. Inflation in that period averaged 2%. That is, a home buyer then would have had a net interest cost 2% higher than a similar buyer today—even with very high current mortgage rates.

Further, the additional interest resulting from a higher rate may be more than offset by the rapid appreciation of the property purchased with the net loan proceeds. If you wait for lower interest rates, you will forgo that appreciation of your new properties and, in addition, have to pay more for properties you purchase in the future. The reduction in interest charges is minor compared to the appreciation lost and for which you must now pay. And, again, remember that these interest charges are deductible.

Note that you can also use an equity loan secured by a second trust deed/mortgage to accomplish the same pyramiding objectives.

In this situation, however, the first trust deed/mortgage and its corollary indebtedness remains intact, and a new trust deed/mortgage (and resulting debt) is established. Therefore, in the aforementioned example, you have a first trust deed on the property and still owe $45,000 on the debt. The value of the house is $100,000. Most lenders will permit an equity loan of up to approximately 80% of the value of the house less the existing debt. At the 80% figure, you would obtain an equity loan of $35,000 (the same amount of net proceeds in a true refinancing), secured by a second trust deed/mortgage on the property. The equity loan may be more attractive depending on interest rates and the availability of funds.

27

Tax-Free Exchange

An exchange of your real properties held for productive use in a trade or business (and you are in this trade or business) or held for investment will yield very favorable tax results. No gain or loss is recognized (even though you realize a gain/loss) on the exchange if you trade your property solely for property of "like-kind," to be held for similar purposes. This does not mean that income taxes will never be owing, but that they are indefinitely postponed until you sell the exchanged property at a price exceeding the adjusted basis, or possibly to death—and then there will be no income tax due. (See Chapter 25.)

Like-Kind Exchanges

What do the words *like-kind* mean? They refer to the nature or character of the property, *not* its grade or quality. Thus, real property cannot be exchanged for personal property. These words (like-kind) are subject to a broad interpretation in the case of exchanges of real property. Some examples of like-kind real property exchanges that have been approved include urban real property for a ranch or farm; a rental house for a store building; unimproved real property (land only) for improved real property (land with a building); an oil and gas lease for a ranch (but not including the residence). Note that both properties must qualify. Also note that a trade of your personal residence for another property does *not* constitute a like-kind exchange, since your personal residence is not held for productive use in a trade or business and is not held for investment according to the Internal Revenue Service. (However, refer to the Overview for rules regarding trading your residence for another.)

What is *nonqualifying property?* This includes stock in trade or other property held primarily for sale (inventory), stocks, bonds, notes, securities, and other evidences of debt or evidences of ownership interest. It is permissible for nonqualifying property to be involved in the total transaction, but not to the exclusion of some qualifying property on both sides of the exchange. If, in an exchange, nonqualifying property is also received, it is treated as "boot."

Boot

Boot includes money (including liabilities assumed or attached to the property received), nonqualifying property, and qualifying property that is not of like-kind. Money and debt are taken at face value, while other categories of boot are taken at fair market value. Liabilities such as mortgages are netted to determine the amount of boot received, and only reduction in liabilities is "boot."

If you realize a gain on the exchange, *and* "boot" is received, the gain must be recognized up to the fair market value of the "boot". Note that realization of the gain is not the critical element; *recognition* is. When a gain is *recognized* it is taxable. You should also be aware that receipt of "boot" will *not* cause the recognition of loss in the exchange. Losses are never recognized in like-kind exchanges, regardless of a receipt of boot. Therefore, losses in this type of exchange are not deductible. To ensure a loss deduction, you should sell the property and then buy another property with the proceeds.

An example will help to explain. Assume that you own a building with an adjusted basis of $60,000, valued at $100,000, on which there is a $40,000 mortgage. You then exchange your building for Mr. A's building valued at $70,000, which has a $20,000 mortgage on it, $5,000 in cash, and stocks with a fair market value of $5,000. The boot you have received is the following:

(1) Cash	$ 5,000
(2) Stocks	5,000
(3) Reduction in liabilities	20,000
($40,000 − $20,000)	
Total "boot"	$30,000

(Taxation of the boot depends on whether any realization of gain occurred in the exchange.)

To compute the gain, the following figures will assist:

Amount of Mr. A's building		$ 70,000
Cash		5,000
Stocks		5,000
Mortgage on your building traded		40,000
Total received		$120,000
Less: Adjusted basis of your building	$60,000	
Mortgage assumed by you	20,000	(80,000)
Gain realized on the exchange[a]		$ 40,000

[a]If you had sold the building, this is the amount of gain you would have realized and recognized:

Fair market value	$100,000
Less: Basis	60,000
Gain realized (and recognized)	$ 40,000

Recognition of Gain

How much of this realized gain is recognized and, therefore, taxable? Gain must be recognized up to the fair market value of the boot. Total boot in this case amounts to $30,000 and this, therefore, is the amount of gain recognized. The remaining $10,000 of realized gain ($40,000 realized gain less the $30,000 boot) is *tax-free*. Whether the gain is treated as long-term capital gain and eligible for favorable tax treatment, depends on how long the property has been held. If the holding period exceeds one year, then long-term capital gains treatment should apply, and only 40% of the $30,000 recognized gain (or $12,000) is subject to federal income tax at your marginal rate.

Basis

What is your new basis in the property received? Your new basis in the building you received is your old basis in the building you transferred, plus any gain recognized, minus any loss recognized on boot property transferred, minus the amount of money or other boot received. In this case:

Basis in the building received (Mr. A's original building):

Basis of property transferred		$60,000
Plus: Gain recognized		30,000
Subtotal		$90,000
Less: Boot Received		
(1) Cash	$ 5,000	
(2) Stocks	5,000	
(3) Reduction in liabilities	20,000	(30,000)
Basis in building received		$60,000

Your basis in the building you received remains at the $60,000 figure (which is the same as the basis in the property you transferred).

Holding Period

What is the holding period of the acquired property? Since the property transferred is a trade or business property and the acquired property has the same basis (this can be in whole or in part) as that of the property transferred, the holding period of the acquired property includes the holding period of the property transferred in the exchange. For example, if you had held your building for two years prior to the exchange, the holding period of the property you acquired (originally Mr. A's property) would include this two year period. This could be critical if one of the exchanging parties was short of the one year period and had recognized gain on the exchange or wanted to sell immediately after the exchange, because the favorable long-term capital gains tax treatment depends on the holding period (at least one year).

In the program outlined in other parts of this guide, properties are to be held for at least one year. This is important, because in a sale, exchange, or conversion of real property held less than one year, *all* depreciation is subject to being recaptured as ordinary income. While this Code provision will not concern you because of the long-term nature of your holding period, another recapture provision should be carefully understood in exchange situations.

Depreciation Recapture

In any situation where one depreciable real property is exchanged for another depreciable real property *and accelerated depreciation has been utilized,* there could be depreciation recapture as discussed in Part 2. The maximum recapture gain in an exchange of residential rental buildings (which is treated as ordinary income) would be the greater of (a) the amount of gain recognized on the exchange (because of the receipt of boot) or (b) the additional depreciation amount over straight-line in excess of the fair market value of the property received in the exchange. Note that you may not be subject to any depreciation recapture *even if* you had held this property less than one year and/or you had utilized accelerated depreciation methods. The key here is to make sure that the fair market value of the depreciable real property received is equal to or exceeds the potential recapture gain on the depreciable real property you transferred. If it does, there is no depreciation recapture to worry about.

Multi-Party Exchanges

Multi-party exchanges can, and often do, occur since it is not that common that two parties are mutually interested in each other's property and wish to make an exchange. Take a typical three party exchange for example. Suppose that you want to exchange your property for Mr. Y's property. However, while Mr. Y wants to dispose of his property, he does not want to make an exchange. Instead, Mr. Y wants to sell his property and cash out. You locate Mr. Z and make an agreement with him that you will exchange your property for Mr. Y's, if Mr. Z will buy Mr. Y's property first. Therefore, in back-to-back escrows, Mr. Z pays into escrow #1 the agreed purchase price for Mr. Y's property, to be conveyed to Mr. Z simultaneously with the closing of escrow #2. In escrow #2, you deposit the deed to your property made in favor of Mr. Z, to be effective upon Mr. Z's delivery of the deed to Mr. Y's property made in your favor in escrow #2.

Alternatively, you and Mr. Y could exchange properties with the understanding that Mr. Z will purchase your former property from Mr. Y. Again, two simultaneous escrows are utilized.

Now everyone is happy. You have Mr. Y's property by means of a tax-free exchange. Mr. Y has sold his property and received the cash he desired. As far as Mr. Y is concerned, the transaction is a taxable sale, but remember he wanted to cash out and did so by means of a sale. Mr. Z has your property which he desired.

The mechanics of these and more sophisticated exchanges should be left to professionals because the consequences are extreme. Instead of a tax-free exchange, you, by not following the rules exactly, could have a taxable sale. As a further word of caution, if you want to structure a deal as an exchange, you should clearly state in all documents that the parties are planning such a transaction. This may assist you in a court challenge, since *form* has meant as much or more than *substance* in the recent court decisions involving exchanges.

Advantages/Disadvantages of Exchanges

Why have I dwelled on this type of disposition? I have done so for two primary reasons. The first, as I alluded to earlier, is that the rules must be strictly followed. Otherwise, you gain nothing for all your effort. Second, the benefits from an exchange are tremendous. You have postponed the income taxes due—maybe forever. So, in effect, it is the equivalent of borrowing the amount of taxes that would have been owing (had there been a sale) on an interest-free basis. Having all of your funds intact, you can use the total value of your old property for acquisition of other properties. In this manner, you can accumulate a larger net worth much quicker.

It is true that your depreciation deductions available after an exchange are less than if you had sold the property. This is so because the resulting basis in an exchange is less than that if the property were sold. Remember, in a traditional sale, in most cases, the basis is the cost of the property, whereas in an exchange the basis in the property received may be the same low adjusted basis which the other exchanging party had. These lower depreciation deductions should not overly concern you since the rapid appreciation in properties purchased with the additional funds available after an exchange may more than offset these deductions. Second, if your taxable income is at a low enough point, these deductions are not as useful to you.

Why don't all investors use the exchange device? First, many think exchanges are too complicated and they don't understand them. They are not, although professionals experienced in these matters should be employed. (There are many of these people.) Second, many believe that if they re-invest in another property within two years, they won't owe any income tax on the transaction.

However, this rule unfortunately only applies to your principal residence. For other property, if you do not exchange but use a sale device, you will pay income taxes if there is a gain. It is that simple. Third, many real estate brokers are unfamiliar with exchanges and mistakenly believe that their commission will be no larger in an exchange as opposed to a sale of the property. However, since taxes are deferred in an exchange, more of the client's equity is preserved. Thus, the client can trade up to a more expensive property. The result is that the real estate commission could be significantly larger.

Finally, many feel that the exchange is just an interesting maneuver, an oddity, but certainly not very common. This is not so. Investors in the western United States, in particular, exchange real property all the time. And, to facilitate these exchanges, an exchange floor has been established in San Francisco (the American Real Estate Exchange or "Amrex" for short). Its function is similar to the New York Stock Exchange. Amrex lists the properties and makes this list available to its members (1,400 to 1,500) for a fee. There is a trading floor of 10,000 square feet where for 12 years properties valued at $250,000 and up have been exchanged. Last year, billions of dollars of properties were listed. To meet the minimum amount, persons owning residential properties have often combined their properties into a package. This is what I envision in our program if you exchange your houses at some date.

You may wish to utilize refinancing/equity loans in conjunction with the exchange vehicle. Prior to the exchange, you might want to borrow additionally on your property. This gives you additional funds tax-free to work with, along with the deductions for the interest generated.

28

Land Lease

In Chapter 2, I discussed the concept of the land lease in terms of a method to break into home ownership. It can also be used as a dispositive device for a person owning both land and building, who later seeks to properly dispose of the property.

Let's assume your rental property has appreciated greatly and most of the depreciation available on the building has been used up. Thus, in a sale, the prospect is a large capital gain. Without a sale, your tax shelter benefit (due to the low amounts of depreciation still available) has been reduced sharply. You would also like a continuous stream of income flowing into your pocket from your investment in this property.

Your solution is to sell the building on an installment sale basis and lease the land to the buyer of the building. Only the gain attributable to the building is taxable (and only part of that each year-see "Installment Sale," Chapter 27). At the same time, the land would be contributing income to you in the form of ground rent. Furthermore, you may be able to borrow against the land and thus obtain tax-free loan proceeds to use for other purposes (see Chapter 26). In this way, you have been able to use the land appreciation.

Note: Your (the lessor's) protection regarding payment on the lease is that the lessee knows that on a default, he would lose his investment. You would repossess the building and be entitled to retain all rent payments paid to date. Also note that you would be able to counter inflationary effects by incorporating into the ground lease a provision that stipulates periodic land appraisals. Since the ground rent is a percentage of the land value, an increasing appraised value would thus lead to an increasing ground rent. This is exactly the history of the land-lease situation, although intervals between re-appraisals should be reasonable (for example, every five years).

The last twist with this device is that you could devise your land to your heirs and no one would even incur any income tax on the gain in value (see "Devise," Chapter 25).

29

Joint Tenancy

Joint tenancy is not often thought of as a method of disposition but rather as a way to hold title, as discussed in Chapter 6. However, as previously mentioned in that chapter, property held as joint tenancy with right of survivorship avoids probate upon the death of the first joint tenant. *Probate* is a court proceeding used to clear title to property passing under the will or by intestacy. It is a matter of public record and normally involves various costs and delays.

However, joint tenancy as a dispositive device may have some merit in certain instances. When the taxpayer dies, the other joint tenant is automatically the holder of the complete interest in that property. No income tax has been imposed on this automatic transfer. There may be some estate taxes, since the proportion owned by the decedent will be included in his gross estate. In the case of spousal joint tenants, the estate of the first to die will include one-half of the value of the property, regardless of which spouse furnished the consideration for the property. State inheritance taxes may or may not be a factor. You should note the basis adjustment upon the death of a joint tenant, as described in Part I.

Joint tenancy does have its drawbacks. First, there can be gift tax consequences for nonspousal joint tenants if one of the joint tenants uses his own separate funds, pays the entire sum for the property, or pays more than his proportionate share. Second, the joint tenant gives up his right of testamentary disposition. (He can't will his interest to others.) Third, holding the property in this way does not allow each of the joint tenants to leave his share of the property in such a way as to save other taxes. For example, the survivor may already have a large gross estate and does not need more property; it only increases estate taxes. Fourth, the survivor may not need additional income that this property provides; this will only increase that burden. Fifth, the probate avoidance feature of joint tenancy can now also be enjoyed by those holding title as community property (at least in California). Finally, only the decedent joint tenant's one-half interest is given a step-up in basis upon his death, as opposed to both halves in the case of community property. This is very important upon the sale of the property. In the case of the joint tenancy property, the taxable gain will be much larger. Thus, in light of these drawbacks, joint tenancy must be carefully scrutinized beforehand in conjunction with your personal financial circumstances.

30

Special Considerations

Some words of caution are in order. You should not sell to or exchange your depreciable property with "related persons"—at least if reducing taxes is a concern. *Related persons* (if there is a gain) are defined as:

1. Husband and wife.
2. A taxpayer and a partnership or corporation that is 80% owned by the taxpayer and/or his spouse.
3. Partnerships and corporations that are 80% owned by the taxpayer and/or spouse.

If you do sell to or exchange your depreciable property with a related person, any gain recognized will generally be treated as *ordinary* income, thus destroying the possibility of receiving the favorable capital gains treatment. This rule exists to prohibit related persons from recognizing a gain at favorable capital gains rates for the purpose of increasing depreciation deductions against ordinary income. (The related person would have a new increased basis (his cost) from which to measure depreciation deductions.)

Note also in the case of a sale or exchange of depreciable property between "related persons" (as defined above) that the installment method of treating gain is generally not available.

If there is a loss in a transaction (sale/exchange) between related taxpayers, very likely no deduction will be allowed for such loss. If this situation applies to you, you should consult an attorney, since special rules and definitions (e.g., "related taxpayers") apply.

In addition, in regard to the operation of your rental properties, you will want to structure your activities so as to lead to your characterization (upon disposition of a property) as an "investor" as opposed to a "dealer." An *investor* is a taxpayer who holds property primarily for investment or for use in a trade or business. A *dealer* is a taxpayer who holds property primarily for sale in the course of business.

Why is this critical? Aside from other tax considerations, this designation may affect tax treatment of the sale of the property. A dealer generally will report his sales as ordinary gain/loss. However, an investor's sales generally will give rise to either capital gain/ capital loss, or capital gain/ordinary loss treatment (depending on whether the asset was held for production of income or for use in a trade or business). In addition, the investor has available to him the provisions of the tax-free exchange section of the Code, something that is expressly denied to the dealer.

Note, however, that merely characterizing yourself as an investor or dealer does not necessarily protect you from being treated otherwise. For any particular piece of property, the inquiry must go further. The basis question to be answered is: what was your *primary purpose* of holding the property *at the time of acquisition?* Some factors to consider in answering this question include the following:

1. The frequency, volume, degree of continuity, and regularity of your real property transactions.
2. The degree to which you have been involved in activities such as subdividing, plotting, improving, and developing the property.
3. The extent of your sales effort in the disposition of the property.
4. The length of time for which the property has been held, and time period between its acquisition and disposition.
5. The extent of your non-real property income activities and the actual amount of time spent on these activities.
6. The extent of your income from real property transactions compared to that derived from other activities.

7. Any membership in a dealer association.

8. How you classified yourself/your business on your tax return, stationery, telephone listing, etc..

9. Whether the property was formerly used (before the disposition) in your trade or business.

10. Whether the property was income-producing.

It is true, as a general rule, that property held primarily for use in your rental trade or business results in capital gain/ordinary loss upon sale. However, increase your protection of this tax status by following the tips previously mentioned in Part II (see Chapter 12) and elsewhere in this guide. In addition, it would be wise to reflect your intention to use these properties on a long-term basis in a rental trade or business in written documents—not only in the purchase documents but also in memos and notes written between you and your real estate agent/broker. Clear and complete records of rental income and expenses should be kept. You should avoid frequent sales/exchanges of your properties. You should hold your properties for an adequate period of time before disposing of them. You should be able to explain the dispositions in terms of economic need or some other reason not related to a mere desire to buy and sell real estate at a profit.

To protect any real property transaction, a tax/real estate attorney should be consulted before proceeding.

Further, vacation homes have not been discussed at any point, since separate rules may apply to these properties. Also, if you live in a state other than California, you should be aware that different tax ramifications may accrue, and other state laws may alter the program outlined in this guide. You should consult professionals in your area.

Final Comments

We have seen a true tax shelter arrangement in operation. By *leveraging* the property (most of the funds involved came from others in the form of a mortgage loan), you have been able to lower the initial cash cost of your investment, thereby increasing the rate of return on the property. Second, use of the "paper" deduction, *depreciation*, has helped to offset a significant amount of gross income, which would have been taxed at ordinary income rates. Note that you receive large depreciation deduction for a relatively small cost (the down payment). The deduction might amount to several times the cash put down on the purchase. Third, upon disposition of the property, **ordinary income has been converted to long-term capital gain** (if any gain is recognized at all on the disposition), which receives very favorable tax treatment.

I tried to make the information contained in this guide as easy to read and understand as possible. Sometimes, that was not possible, and I know that certain sections may be difficult to comprehend. Therefore, I suggest that you reread those sections. After all, as I suggested in the preface, this type of program is going to require some effort. But this extra effort will hopefully be very rewarding.

I sincerely hope that you embark on *some* tax-reduction program, regardless of whether it is this type of program or not. Your financial future may very well depend on how you respond to the current tax environment. In your struggle to reduce your taxes, consult professionals. What may seem like a large fee (if one is charged) for their services now could well be the best money you ever spent. Good luck!

P.S. What does Vincent Zucchero do now that this guide is completed? First, I will spend additonal time with my law practice and investment counseling activities. Second, I will continue to write more guides/books, since I believe that I can convey additional information that could be helpful to others. Third, I expect that my activities as General Counsel and Vice-President, Asset Management of a large real estate syndication and development firm will increase over time.

I enjoyed writing this guide and would like to hear your comments. Thanks.

Index